**New Directions for
Adult and Continuing
Education**

Susan Imel
Jovita M. Ross-Gordon
COEDITORS-IN-CHIEF

MW01221719

Reaching Out
Across the Border:
Canadian Perspectives
in Adult Education

Patricia Cranton
Leona M. English
EDITORS

Number 124 • Winter 2009
Jossey-Bass
San Francisco

REACHING OUT ACROSS THE BORDER: CANADIAN PERSPECTIVES IN
ADULT EDUCATION
Patricia Cranton and Leona M. English (eds.)
New Directions for Adult and Continuing Education, no. 124
Susan Imel, Jovita M. Ross-Gordon, Coeditors-in-Chief

Microfilm copies of issues and articles are available in 16mm and 35mm,
as well as microfiche in 105mm, through University Microfilms Inc., 300
North Zeeb Road, Ann Arbor, Michigan 48106-1346.

NEW DIRECTIONS FOR ADULT AND CONTINUING EDUCATION (ISSN 1052-2891,
electronic ISSN 1536-0717) is part of The Jossey-Bass Higher and Adult Education Series and is published quarterly by Wiley Subscription Services, Inc.,
A Wiley Company, at Jossey-Bass, 989 Market Street, San Francisco, California 94103-1741. Periodicals Postage Paid at San Francisco, California, and
at additional mailing offices. POSTMASTER: Send address changes to New
Directions for Adult and Continuing Education, Jossey-Bass, 989 Market
Street, San Francisco, California 94103-1741.

New Directions for Adult and Continuing Education is indexed in CIJE: Cur-
rent Index to Journals in Education (ERIC); Contents Pages in Education
(T&F); ERIC Database (Education Resources Information Center); Higher
Education Abstracts (Claremont Graduate University); and Sociological
Abstracts (CSA/CIG).

SUBSCRIPTIONS cost $98.00 for individuals and $269.00 for institutions,
agencies, and libraries.

EDITORIAL CORRESPONDENCE should be sent to the Coeditors-in-Chief, Susan
Imel, ERIC/ACVE, 1900 Kenny Road, Columbus, Ohio 43210-1090,
e-mail: imel.l@osu.edu; or Jovita M. Ross-Gordon, Southwest Texas State
University, EAPS Dept., 601 University Drive, San Marcos, TX 78666.

Cover photograph by Jack Hollingsworth@Photodisc

www.josseybass.com

Contents

EDITORS' NOTES

In proposing this New Directions volume, we wondered how to articulate our varied historical, geographical, and political positions in our field. As a point of reference we asked what we might say to our U.S. or U.K. colleagues about our uniqueness. Though we have written to and for each other about being Canadian (Selman and others, 1998), this volume provided us with an opportunity to address a broader audience and speak about what is Canadian about Canadian adult education. Our chapter authors have done this by detailing our history, our educational initiatives, our movements, and our linguistic struggles. As with many other such projects, including defining what adult education means and is, we were at times tempted to default to what we are not: we are not American, we are not public school educators, and so on. Instead, the chapter authors have moved to a more positive articulation of concerns, interests, and discourses—to a naming of what we are and what we have been concerned with.

In 2005, I (Patricia Cranton) had the wonderful opportunity to become visiting professor of adult education at Penn State Harrisburg. I was excited about working in a doctoral program and with colleagues I had long admired: Daniele Flannery, Edward Taylor, and Elizabeth Tisdell. Like most other Canadian adult educators, I had regularly attended conferences in the United States, read the literature from U.S. scholars, and was familiar with the theory and practice of adult education in the United States. However, I learned that U.S. scholars and doctoral students were less familiar with Canadian adult education—our history, our philosophy, our projects, and our literature.

In 2007, the Adult Education Research Conference was held jointly with the Canadian Association for the Study of Adult Education Conference in Halifax, Canada. My Penn State colleagues and I attended that conference, along with a group of our doctoral students who were enrolled in a special independent study course to learn from conference sessions. Ed Taylor and I facilitated this course and chose a Canadian theme for the students' preconference and postconference readings and papers. Some students were able to participate in a preconference workshop held at St. Francis Xavier University in Antigonish, Nova Scotia, and the Coady Institute at the university. These events reinforced, in my mind, the need for Canadian adult educators to communicate our work to our U.S. colleagues.

In Chapter One, Donovan Plumb writes about the emergence and development of critical adult education discourses in Canada since the founding of the Canadian Association for the Study of Adult Education in 1935. Plumb

NEW DIRECTIONS FOR ADULT AND CONTINUING EDUCATION, no. 124, Winter 2009 © 2009 Wiley Periodicals, Inc.
Published online in Wiley InterScience (www.interscience.wiley.com) • DOI: 10.1002/ace.347

1

points to the relationship we adult educators in Canada have had with critical theory and with a critical perspective and how we have used these to strengthen our analysis and our practice. Plumb points to the many intellectual influences on our thinking and our preoccupations in this field.

In Chapter Two, Suzanne Robinson speaks directly to adult education in Canada's far north, describing innovative efforts to use video and dialogue to promote and celebrate adult and literacy education. Robinson's project is one of many that fit into our history of using media as a means of traversing distance with a far-flung northern population comprising primarily of our underserved First Nations people. Her work is unique, and it shows how difficult it is to negotiate community development projects in a northern area.

Taking a historical perspective in Chapter Three, Dorothy MacKeracher highlights four social learning movements that developed in Canada in the early twentieth century. She brings special attention to the role of women in Frontier College, the Women's Institutes, the Antigonish movement, and the United Farmers of Canada (Saskatchewan) and makes it clear that our field's commitment has been to serving the underprivileged and advancing the social welfare of our citizens.

No discussion of Canada would be complete without attention to the way in which adult education has evolved and grown in the French province of Quebec. Despite being a bilingual country, English and French colleagues do not always know what is happening in each linguistic sector, so we suspect many Canadian colleagues will find Mohamed Hrimech's chapter on this topic informative too. In Chapter Four he articulates some of the special issues that define Quebec: its attention to language and linguistic rights and the role of adult education and training in the survival of the language and the culture and in strengthening the economy. He provides a thorough exploration of an adult education sector that is immersed fully in the political and economic realities of a bilingual province.

In Chapter Five, Allan Quigley and his colleagues make the links between health and adult literacy, reporting on research with the federal Health and Learning Knowledge Centre in which they sought to establish the effects of low literacy on health, access to health care, and the provision of adequate health services. The authors highlight the issue that despite the enviable Canadian health care system, our population has trouble accessing it because of low levels of literacy. Concerns with literacy and health have increasingly come to the fore in adult education circles in Canada, and this chapter shows the learning challenges that are implicit in the system.

In Chapter Six, Elizabeth Lange and Aaron Chubb explore environmental student activism on campuses in both Canada and the United States, concluding that Canada faces a critical decision to move from environmentally debilitative economics to become what they term "a global leader in creating a sustainable society." This chapter points to our somewhat troubling history of environmental responsiveness and suggests some ways forward.

In our Canadian higher education system, the community college plays a decidedly important role. In Chapter Seven, Ellen Carusetta and Patricia Cranton present a case study within which faculty development is treated as an adult education initiative. They point to the number of adult educators who are employed in our community college system and explore the creative ways in which teaching and learning are facilitated in the colleges.

In Chapter Eight, Leona English offers an account of major emphases in adult education for community development. She discusses four features in Canada: focus on adult learning, use of media and the arts, international initiatives, and feminist leanings. Although each of these features alone is not distinctive, together they present a unique picture of how adult education and community development have become entwined in a project of national change and growth.

As we discuss in Chapter Nine, adult education in Canada is unique in some respects and the same as the United States in others. This is to be expected given our shared land mass, our entwined economies, and the strong presence of the U.S. media in Canada. We hope that this volume serves to introduce our U.S. colleagues to Canadian perspectives in adult education and helps inform their practice, their research, and their studies.

Patricia Cranton
Leona M. English
Editors

Reference

Selman, G., Cooke, M., Selman, M., and Dampier, P. *The Foundations of Adult Education in Canada*. (2nd ed.) Toronto: Thompson Educational Publishing, 1998.

PATRICIA CRANTON *is professor of adult education at Penn State University Harrisburg.*

LEONA M. ENGLISH *is professor of adult education at St. Francis Xavier University in Antigonish, Nova Scotia.*

1

This chapter describes the emergence and development of critical adult education discourses in Canada since the founding of the Canadian Association for the Study of Adult Education.

Critical Adult Education in Canada in the Time of CASAE

Donovan Plumb

From very early in its history, the Canadian Association for the Study of Adult Education (CASAE) has supported a rich tradition of critique. This chapter argues, however, that in important ways, the magnitude and rapidity of social transformations since the late 1970s have largely overwhelmed the critical capacities of Canadian adult educators. In particular, drawing on recent work by Boltanski and Chiapello (2005), I suggest that critical adult education in Canada has been one-sided. Contemporary social forms have primarily been criticized for the ways they generate inauthenticity or deepen cultural forms of oppression (described below as "artistic critique") than for the ways they deepen poverty or enchance egotism ("social critique"). As a result, the relationship of adult education to some of the most serious harms generated by recent forms of network capitalism remains insufficiently explored.

Uneasy in '82

On May 8, 1982, Canadian adult educator Michael Collins went to bed disgruntled. Election results were in, and the Progressive Conservative party of Saskatchewan, led by Grant Devine, had won a landside victory over the New Democratic party (NDP), ending over a decade of social democratic rule in the province. A staunch leftist, Collins had never felt out of place in Saskatchewan. It was here that the first socialist government in North America, the Cooperative Commonwealth Federation (CCF), was elected in

NEW DIRECTIONS FOR ADULT AND CONTINUING EDUCATION, no. 124, Winter 2009 © 2009 Wiley Periodicals, Inc.
Published online in Wiley InterScience (www.interscience.wiley.com) • DOI: 10.1002/ace.348

1944. In the years before the 1944 election, adult education activism in support of agricultural cooperatives, unions, and other social groups had contributed strongly to the development of the CCF. After it, radical adult educators such as Watson Thompson joined the CCF to develop "grassroots radical adult education" initiatives to support the "enactment of a democratic socialist learning society" (Welton, 2005, pp. 26–27). Three decades later, the vestiges of these efforts were still present. Collins's own rather radical views of adult education, expressed most clearly in his critique of managerialism in adult education (particularly "competency-based education"; Collins, 1987), were not out of place in a context where left-leaning views were often aired.

Collins would not have been overly bothered about Devine's election if it were just a minor shift in the political sentiments of Saskatchewan. This time, however, things seemed more ominous. Devine's election appeared to be part of a much broader political shift. The previous year, Ronald Reagan had become president of the United States and had just fired over eleven thousand striking air traffic controllers after they disobeyed back-to-work legislation. In Britain, Margaret Thatcher was nearing the close of her first term, in which she had cut spending on social programs, attacked British unions, and privatized government industries. On the Canadian national stage, Pierre Trudeau's Liberals were in trouble in the polls, and the Progressive Conservatives, touting Thatcher's rhetoric of restraint and cutbacks, could barely wait for the next election. Again and again, the mantra was repeated: the socialist aspirations of the left were politically and economically impossible; further prosperity could be achieved only if the economy was set free from the dead weight of the welfare state.

The uneasiness Collins felt that night turned out to be well founded. In the following decade, governments around the world largely disassembled the edifice of the welfare state. Faced with declining union participation, the fall of the Berlin wall, the privatization of public industries, and burgeoning consumerism and individualization, any residual hope for socialism seemed naive. Francis Fukuyama (1989) triumphantly declared that this was the "end of history" (p. 2). The "universalization of Western liberal democracy," he argued, marked a veritable "end point of mankind's ideological evolution" (1992, p. 271). Perhaps as a sign of the times, at the 1990 Commission of Professors in Adult Education, Collins was derided for his leftist views after he challenged the commission to take a stand and reject any suggestion that adult education was "selling out to the corporate ethos of big business" (Collins, 1990, p. 4). In 1991, he tried a different tack, suggesting it was not just leftist ideals that were being trammeled by neoconservatism but liberal ideals as well. "Liberals and socialists are in general agreement about the need for justice and equality," he would argue. "Rather than taking digs at the 'left,' then, we would be more relevantly engaged in working out our responses to ten years of radical neo-conservative assault on the values we espouse in adult education" (Collins, 1991, p. 4).

As it would turn out, Collins's appeal to liberal values involved a significant misreading of the nature of the changes that were taking place in society. Over the next decade, the actions of so-called third way liberal, labor, and social democratic governments (Bill Clinton in the United States, Tony Blair in Britain, Jean Chrétien in Canada, and even the NDP under Roy Romanow in Saskatchewan) revealed that the social changes happening were not simply the result of neoconservatism, but a much more pervasive neoliberal transformation aimed to free markets from state encumbrances. The transformation rippling across the world entailed the consolidation of an unprecedented flexible and mobile form of network capitalism. The change from industrial to network capitalism was so massive and rapid that it virtually defied understanding. Critical resources that previously had provided the left with some capacity to wring accommodation from the capitalist nation state suddenly had no purchase. Michael Collins was certainly not alone in his struggle to understand and respond to the great changes that were sweeping society and, along with it, the entire field of adult education.

The Canadian Association for the Study of Adult Education

Just when the dramatic shifts of network capitalism were manifesting for the first time on the political stage, a contingent of academics in Canada formed the Canadian Association for the Study of Adult Education (CASAE) in 1981. Largely as a result of the earlier work of advocates such as Ned Corbett, Roby Kidd, and Alan Thomas involved with the Canadian Association for Adult Education, by the early 1980s, academic adult education was well established in Canadian universities. A growing number of professors claimed adult education as their primary area of teaching and research. Numerous graduate education programs (including Ph.D. programs in adult education at University of British Columbia, Ontario Institute for Studies in Education, and Université de Montreal) were supporting the education of a diverse range of students (Draper, 1974).

Just as in the United States, adult education in Canada persisted as a relatively small and marginalized academic field. Although there was little doubt about the practical achievements of adult educators in Canada, there was concern that the field did not possess strong academic standing. As André Grace (2000) relates, for instance, Roby Kidd, a central figure in Canadian adult education during the middle decades of the 20th century, "believed that the main opposition to the enterprise [of adult education] . . . was due, in part, to a perceived lack of concern with educational standards in adult education" (p. 151). Adult education programs, even at the graduate level, focused more on practice than theory. Research in the field drew heavily (but rather thinly) on psychological theories in an attempt to distinguish adult learning as a domain warranting specific investigation and to assert adult education as a professional field requiring its own contingent of academic researchers. For many, Alan Tough's well-received research on "adult learning projects" (1971) pointed the way forward for Canadian academic adult education. Canada had an important contribution to make to the field of adult education. To support this potential, Canadian professors and students of adult education needed a separate forum where they could share research, explore theories, and address adult education issues unique to Canada.

Thus, perhaps more than anything else, it was aspirations to professionalization, not any particular critical agenda, that drove the formation of CASAE. However, Canadian academics of adult education, perhaps as a way to distinguish themselves from their neighbors to the south (a constant concern for Canadians in general), maintained a proud attachment to their historical adult education heritage. But their purpose was pragmatic: to improve the standing of academic adult education researchers in Canada through the establishment of an organization that could foster and showcase Canadian academic research. And for the first several years, this seemed precisely what CASAE managed to accomplish.

CASAE and the Challenge of Critique

While CASAE did indeed become a productive organization, its trajectory by the late 1980s was curving in a direction largely unanticipated by its founding members. Rather than becoming a context within which adult education researchers would develop theoretical support for the view of adult education as professional andragogical practice in line with what was occurring in the United States, especially under the broad umbrella of the American Association for Adult and Continuing Education, CASAE gradually evolved as a discursive context increasingly critical of adult education as an individualized and professionalized practice. As early as 1985, in a symposium presided over by Adèle Chené, academic adult educators explored the relationship between ideology and adult education (Chené, 1985).

While the discourses of CASAE were often critical of prevailing individualistic notions of adult education, the perspectives informing these discourses were far from unified. In fact, a fundamental attribute of Canadian academic adult education over the past two decades has been the plethora of critical perspectives its varied theorists hold on the modern practice of adult education. French sociologists Luc Boltanski and Eve Chiapello (2005) offer important insight into why this might have been so. The capitalist nation-state has undergone such a massive and rapid shift over the past three decades, moving from an industrial to a network form, that it has largely outstripped its resources for critique. The changes have left intellectuals and activists flogging about, trying to gain a critical understanding of our world. Only now, with the broad dimensions of this new form of global network capitalism finally consolidating, are systematic critiques emerging

New Directions for Adult and Continuing Education • DOI: 10.1002/ace

(and I would place Boltanski and Chiapello's among the best of these). CASAE's fortuitous constitution at the very moment of interregnum, when states around the world began the staggering quarter-century task of transforming the social infrastructure to support networked capitalism, left Canadian academic adult educators struggling to come to terms with the role of adult education. While it is impossible to provide a complete account of the myriad threads that formed the fabric of critical adult education discourse in Canada over these years, it is useful to highlight some of its prominent lineaments.

Sources of Indignation

Boltanski and Chiapello (2005) offer a useful frame for understanding the varied critical discourses present in CASAE over the past decades. They contend that at bottom, critique is always driven by indignation, a largely emotional and affective reaction people feel in response to suffering. Over the past two hundred years, capitalism has evoked four principal kinds of indignation:

1. Indignation in response to the way capitalism results in the "disenchantment" of the world and in the "inauthenticity" and meaninglessness of objects, people, and social structures it generates
2. Indignation in response to "oppression" of people under its influence, particularly as they are subjected to its work regimes and to the varied and shifting cultural and social forms (the bourgeois family, racist social relations, fascist regimes, and so on) that it spawns and supports
3. Indignation in response to the "poverty" that it inevitably produces
4. Indignation in response to "opportunism and egotism" that promotes the breakdown of caring relations and social solidarity (p. 37)

Boltanski and Chiapello argue that these sources of indignation have motivated two general forms of critique: artistic critique and social critique (p. 38). Artistic critique, expressed most clearly in bohemianism, is mostly fed by the first two sources of indignation. The primary concern is with the ways capitalism suppresses authentic expression; disenchants nature and culture; imposes mechanistic, hierarchical, and oppressive social and cultural patterns; disrupts the fruition of human capacity; and homogenizes individual and cultural differences. Social critique, developed most fully in Marxism, is driven by the last two sources of indignation. The major issue here is with the ways capitalist relations result in exploitation that leads to inequity and impoverishment, on the one hand, and to egotism, greed, instrumentalism, wastefulness, and hard-heartedness, on the other. Although both artistic critique and social critique are critical of capitalism, given the very different nature of their underlying sources of indignation, they often find themselves in conflict.

New Directions for Adult and Continuing Education • DOI: 10.1002/ace

Critical Lineaments

Indignation in response to disenchantment, inauthenticity, and oppression quickly grew in the newly formed CASAE. While I doubt Michael Collins would identify too easily with the term *artistic critique,* his early criticism of competency-based education largely emerged from his concern with the way this educational technology threatened the authentic learning engagements of humans-in-the-world. Collins argued that competency-based education failed to recognize humans as intentional beings embedded with others in relations of meaning. Moreover, while many other adult education trends of the 1970s (such as andragogy) were far less intrusive than the much more obviously instrumental example of competency-based education, Collins was keen to point out how the same set of behaviorist assumptions that vastly oversimplified and disenchanted human learning processes underlay most of them.

Collins's critique of competency-based education and other forms of education that aimed to reproduce the skills, knowledge, and attitudes of industrial capitalism accorded with the views of another increasingly influential Canadian adult education academic. Michael Welton certainly agreed with Collins's critique of the limitations of technologies like competency-based education. He differed with Collins, however, on the primary source of his indignation with capitalism. For Welton, it was not so much the way capitalist forms of adult education were generating personal inauthenticity, but rather the ways they disrupted social solidarity and supported systems that produced great harms like poverty, inequality, violence, transience, and exploitation. Welton despaired at the abandonment of adult education as a social movement that had prevailed in Canada in the first half of the twentieth century.

Jürgen Habermas's English publication of *Theory of Communicative Action* (1984) deeply affected both Collins and Welton. Given his sources of indignation, Collins drew on Habermas's critique of instrumental rationality to advance his critique of the oppressive effects of purposive-rational adult education (Collins and Plumb, 1989). Given his sources of indignation, Welton drew on Habermas's thesis of capitalism's (economic and state) colonization of the lifeworld to articulate a new basis for reviving adult education as a social movement "in defense of the lifeworld" (Welton, 1995). Both perspectives, very much on the table at the joint AERC (Adult Education Research Conference)/CASAE conference in Calgary in 1988, had a deeply unsettling effect. Largely as a result of Welton's and Collins's critical engagements, meetings in the late 1980s and early 1990s were abuzz with talk of critical theory. Strong critical currents coursing into the field from a variety of other directions variously affirmed or challenged the broad, systematic formulations of Habermasian critical theory.

Feminism was perhaps one of the most important of these. Early on, a contingent of able feminist adult education theorists such as Shawna Butterwick

(1986, 1987), Joyce Stalker (1996), Kathleen Rockhill (1987), and Angela Miles (1985) began to challenge the patriarchal orientation of the field. The source of indignation for these feminist adult educators was the ways capitalist-patriarchal social relations (particularly the bourgeois family) resulted in the oppression of women. While some feminists, such as Patricia Gouthro (2000), acknowledged the capacity of Habermasian critical theory to understand the harm that instrumental rationality caused on the lives of women, they also pointed out the profound gender blindness of critical theory. Theory of communicative action, Gouthro argued, failed to attend to the specific ways that women are oppressed in contemporary society.

Feminism's critique of critical theory accorded with a widening post-modern sensibility that rapidly gained steam in Canadian adult education throughout the 1980s and 1990s. While the influence of postmodern theo-retical perspectives was far less influential in Canadian adult education than they were to become in Britain (Edwards and Usher, 1994), Collard and Law (1990) fairly early on posited some of its critical implications for the field. For the most part, postmodernist critics were indignant with how, in moder-nity, a scientific metanarrative of technological and social progress was resulting in the wholesale systematization and homogenization of society. All of human interaction, it seemed, was being reduced to the commodity form, resulting in the disenchantment (and ultimate destruction) of differ-ent cultures and the oppressive regulation and exclusion of all people and lifestyles deemed incompatible with the metanarratives of modernity. The critique of postmodernism, then, primarily took the form of artistic critique.

Drawing deeply on these sentiments, adult educators in Canada asso-ciated with a proliferating number of new social movements began to engage in widespread critical attacks on the deeply modernist and progres-sivist adult education mainstream in Canada. A good example of this was the increasingly influential lesbian and gay critique of homophobia and het-erosexism in adult education. Over the past fifteen years, André Grace (Grace and Hill, 2004), for instance, has played an active role challenging the heteronormative biases of Canadian adult education theory and prac-tice. Following another tack, Leona English (2000), Tara Fenwick (English, Fenwick, and Parsons, 2003), and Al Lauzon (2001), indignant about the disenchantment and spiritual vacuity of mainstream adult education prac-tices, explored ways that adult education can contribute to deepening capac-ities for spirituality. Their indignation over the disenchanting effects of modern capitalism has been echoed by Darlene Clover (2003), who has focused on the role that adult education can play in the environmental movement. Clover's critique explicitly discusses the recent transformations of capitalism from a nation-based, industrial form to a globalized network form. Her critical sensibilities are expressly artistic in orientation in that they rest primarily on the ways globalized capitalism is destroying the aes-thetic integrity of both indigenous cultures and the natural world that sus-tains them. When looked at through the lens provided by Boltanski and

Chiapello, critical discourses in Canada have primarily taken the form of artistic critique.

Despite its diminished presence, social critique has persisted as a small but important part of critical adult education discourse in Canada. Perhaps one of the most vocal contributors to social critique in CASAE has been Bruce Spencer, whose ongoing interest in unions as a key site of adult learning is directly connected to his own indignation at the inequalities and egotism sustained by capitalism. Over the past thirty years, however, Spencer has witnessed a dramatic demise in unionism in Canada and a gradual waning of discourse in adult education of the importance of unions as a context for the kinds of adult learning that can contest the social destructiveness of capitalism. Drawing our attention to the dramatic inequities, poverty, and violence produced by contemporary capitalism in much of the world, Shahrzad Mojab (1998, 2001) argues that we must once again strive to develop critical resources equal to the transformed circumstances of our age.

Critique in a Context of Networked Capitalism

Capitalism has proven itself masterful at adapting to any critique that threatens its vitality and strength. If one understands capitalism as a process nurtured and protected by legions of owners, workers, politicians, academics, pundits, and so on, this really is not too surprising. In a curious way, its adaptiveness stands as testament to the innovation and creativity of the people who serve it. Since Michael Collins's fitful night in 1982, capitalism has once again shown its power to mutate to meet new circumstances. This time, in response to the economic drag of the welfare state, it has acquired capacities for nimble and timely production. This has entailed a massive transformation in the productive apparatus from one focused on highly centralized and standardized industry to one modeled on distributed and ever changing networks.

For the most part, network capitalism has managed to address (albeit largely in its own attenuated way) some of the major sources of indignation that industrial capitalism provoked. Network capitalism does not confront us in the same way with disenchantment and inauthenticity. In a world of proliferating choice (consumer choice, that is), we are less prone to feel we are deprived of an identity we value. In fact, it is likely that someone is trying very hard to understand what we feel is authentic so it can be packaged somehow and sold to us in the form of a rebellious T-shirt or self-help book.

As important as the development of critique has been in Canadian adult education, without a deep and persistent scrutiny of the ways adult education, even its critical variants, fails to address the ever-transforming source of what causes much of our indignation in contemporary times, we end up incapable of supporting anything but partisan change. Certainly artistic critique is important, but we must not rely on it too much. For while we have bemoaned the disenchantment of our world, inequalities have mounted to levels not seen in a century, egotism has grown in an unchecked frenzy of greed, and global social solidarity has been cast to the wind. Now is the time for Canadian adult educators, in solidarity with others around the world, to take hold of new critical resources with which we can seriously challenge the underlying source of our many feelings of indignation.

References

Boltanski, L., and Chiapello, E. *The New Spirit of Capitalism.* New York: Verso, 2005.

Butterwick, S. "A Comparative Review of Consciousness Raising and Conscientization." In M. Gillen and W. Sinnett (eds.), *Proceedings of the Fifth Annual Conference of the Canadian Association for the Study of Adult Education.* Winnipeg, MB: University of Manitoba, 1986.

Butterwick, S. "Learning Liberation: A Comparative Analysis of Feminist Consciousness Raising and Freire's Conscientization Method." In R. Ingster (ed.), *Proceedings of the 28th Annual Adult Education Research Conference.* Laramie: University of Wyoming, 1987.

Chené, A. "Idéologie et éducation des adultes." In *Proceedings of the Fourth Annual Conference of the Canadian Association for the Study of Adult Education.* Guelph, ON: Canadian Association for the Study of Adult Education, 1985. (ED 349 462)

Clover, D. "Environmental Adult Education: Critique and Creativity in a Globalizing World." In L. H. Hill and D. Clover (eds.), *Environmental Adult Education: Ecological Learning, Theory and Practice for Socioenvironmental Change.* New Directions for Adult and Continuing Education, no. 99. San Francisco: Jossey-Bass, 2003.

Collard, S., and Law, M. "Universal Abandon: Postmodernity, Politics and Adult Education." In P. Kleiber and L. Tisdell (eds.), *Proceedings of the Thirty-First Annual Adult Education Research Conference.* Athens: University of Georgia, 1990.

Collins, M. *Competence in Adult Education: A New Perspective.* Lanham, Md.: University Press of America, 1987.

Collins, M. "Some Observations on the Role of the Commission of Professors." In A. Blunt (ed.), *Proceedings of the 1990 Conference of the Commission of Professors of Adult Education.* Saskatoon: University of Saskatchewan, 1990.

Collins, M. "What Went On at the CPAE Meetings in Salt Lake City (or Did We Dream We Saw Joe Hill Last Year!)." In D. Flannery (ed.), *Proceedings of the 1991 Conference of the Commission of Professors of Adult Education.* Montreal, QC: Université de Montreal, 1991.

Collins, M., and Plumb, D. "Some Critical Thinking About Critical Theory and Its Relevance for Adult Education Practice." In C. Coggins (ed.), *Proceedings of the Thirtieth Annual Adult Education Research Conference.* Madison: University of Wisconsin, 1989.

Draper, J. *Adult Education and Community Development in Canada: A Survey of Post-Secondary Courses and Programs.* Toronto: Ontario Institute for Studies in Education, Department of Education, 1974. (ED 107 902)

Edwards, R., and Usher, R. *Postmodernism and Education.* London: Routledge, 1994.

English, L. "Spiritual Dimensions of Informal Learning." In L. M. English and M. A. Gillen (eds.), *Addressing the Spiritual Dimensions of Adult Learning.* New Directions for Adult and Continuing Education, no. 85. San Francisco: Jossey Bass, 2000.

English, L., Fenwick, T., and Parsons, J. *Spirituality in Adult Education.* Malabar, Fla.: Krieger, 2003.

Fukuyama, F. "The End of History?" *National Interest,* 1989, 16(Summer), 2–18.

Fukuyama, F. *The End of History and the Last Man.* New York: Free Press, 1992.

Gouthro, P. "Globalization, Civil Society, and the Homeplace." *Convergence,* 33(2), 2000, 57–77.

Grace, A. "Canadian and US Adult Learning (1945–1970) and the Cultural Politics and Place of Lifelong Learning. *International Journal of Lifelong Education,* 2000, *19*(2), 141–158.

Grace, A., and Hill, R. "Positioning Queer in Adult Education: Intervening in Politics and Praxis in North America." *Studies in the Education of Adults, 36*(2), 2004, 167–189.

Habermas, J. *The Theory of Communicative Action.* Boston: Beacon Press, 1984.

Lauzon, A. "The Challenges of Spirituality in the Everyday Practice of the Adult Educator." *Adult Learning,* 2001, *12*(3), 4–7.

Miles, A. "Feminism, Equality, and Liberation." *Canadian Journal of Women and the Law,* 1985, *1*(1), 42–68.

Mojab, S. "'Muslim' Women and 'Western' Feminists: The Debate on Particulars and Universals." *Monthly Review: An Independent Socialist Magazine, 50*(7), 1998, 19–21.

Mojab, S. "New Resources for Revolutionary Critical Education." *Convergence, 34*(1), 2001, 118–126.

Rockhill, K. "Gender, Language and the Politics of Literacy." *British Journal of Sociology of Education,* 1987, *8*(2), 153–167.

Stalker, J. "Women and Adult Education: Rethinking Androcentric Research." *Adult Education Quarterly,* 1996, *46*(2), 98–113.

Tough, A. *The Adult's Learning Projects: A Fresh Approach to Theory and Practice in Adult Learning.* Toronto: Ontario Institute for Studies in Education, 1971.

Welton, M. (ed.). *In Defense of the Lifeworld: Critical Perspectives on Adult Learning.* Albany: State University of New York Press, 1995.

Welton, M. *Designing the Just Learning Society: A Critical Inquiry.* Leicester: National Institute of Adult Continuing Education, 2005.

DONOVAN PLUMB *teaches at Mount Saint Vincent University in Halifax, Nova Scotia.*

2

Using video and workshops, participants in the study reported here had the opportunity to share their perceptions, thoughts, and hopes for the future of adult education in the North.

Literacy Lives Here: Using Video and Dialogue to Promote and Celebrate Adult and Literacy Education in the Canadian Western Arctic

Suzanne Robinson

The Canadian North, one of most isolated parts of the world, has been subject to increased scrutiny as a source of untapped oil and gas, a global warming harbinger and casualty, and a center of international sovereignty debate. What is often forgotten is that in addition to a resource bed and a border, the Arctic is first a homeland—a homeland to nations of peoples of whom much has been asked and to whom not much has been given, especially in terms of education and literacy for Aboriginal Northerners. This chapter explores the use of video as a tool to dialogue with Northerners in order to better understand their perspectives on education and literacy. The themes arising from the research provide direction for improving communication, teaching, and research in the North or anywhere else that educational inequality exists. For this chapter, *Northerner* refers to a resident of the Northwest Territories (NWT), half of whom are Aboriginal or indigenous Canadians. *Southern* refers to Southern Canada, below the sixtieth parallel.

Research ethics board permission for this study was obtained, and signed consent forms were collected from each participant.

Refocusing Literacy as a Human Right

The Western Arctic, a region of the Northwest Territories (NWT), is also known as the Beaufort-Delta. Two main Aboriginal groups live in the region: the Inuvialuit, also known as Inuit, and the Gwich'in, a Dene First Nation, as well as smaller numbers of other Aboriginal groups such as the Métis. These comprise approximately 70 percent of the total population. From the Indian Act (1876) and Treaty 11 (1921) to the first oil and gas boom, the federal government has imposed policies on the North, which have directly affected these peoples. Although devolution of power, land claims, and self-government promise change, the standard of living of most Northerners is still far below Canadian norms. Saku and Bone (2000) are direct in noting that "the socio-economic conditions of most Aboriginal Canadians remain at a very deplorable state" (p. 10). Above and beyond the responsibility for the Canadian government to provide education to all Canadians, it has additional obligations to Aboriginal Canadians. In the Western Arctic, Treaty 11 and the Northern land claim processes are contracts with the Canadian government—judiciary agreements in which the government made promises of payment and services for the land that Aboriginal people were required to surrender. Education is one item promised in these agreements. One of the hopes of people in this region is that improved literacy and educational success will serve as a means of improving their lives.

Yet education is failing in the Canadian North. The *International Adult Literacy and Skills Survey* (Organization for Economic Co-Operation and Development, and Statistics Canada, 2000) study confirmed that 69 percent of Aboriginal Northerners scored below level 3 (of 5), the level required by most people for day-to-day activities. Conversely, about 70 percent of non-Aboriginal Northerners scored at level 3 or higher. If 69 percent of Aboriginal Canadians do not have the necessary literacy skills, how can they be full participants in Canadian society? The government of the Northwest Territories (2005) found in its research that fewer than half of Aboriginal students complete high school. In contrast, 87.1 percent of non-Aboriginal students complete high school. Non-Aboriginal Northerners are far more likely to complete postsecondary than Aboriginal Northerners are to complete high school. University graduation rates are 4.6 percent for Aboriginal Northerners compared to 27.7 percent for non-Aboriginal Northerners. The common argument is that the schools are there, so the opportunity is there, Nevertheless, given these statistics, it is clear that educational opportunities are not equitable.

Canada, the United States, and Australia are the only countries in the United Nations not to ratify the Declaration on the Rights of Indigenous Peoples (2007), a strong indication that the Canadian government is not fully committed to righting the inequality of Aboriginal Canadian education and literacy. The wording of Article 15 of the declaration is clear: the United Nations maintains that Indigenous people "have the right to all levels and forms of education of the State . . . in a manner appropriate to their cultural methods of teaching and learning" (p. 6). This is a failure of Canada on a moral, legal, and humanitarian level. Yet this situation in the Arctic is not so very different from the educational reality of American students from poor communities, immigrant communities, and communities of color. The United States has a growing movement that proposes that education is the civil rights issue of our time and for education to be enshrined in the U.S. Constitution. The Canadian Charter of Human Rights and Freedoms does not include education as a fundamental right, a significant oversight given that education and literacy are often the keys to lasting change.

Video as a Tool for Education

There is a deep contrast between the realities of the educational system in the North and the educational hopes of Northerners. An American organization, Quality Education as a Constitutional Right, states on its Web site that these disadvantaged groups "must play a leading role in the vision, formulation, and actualization of the work toward ensuring a high quality public education for all." Video, a powerful teaching tool, is one way to capture and communicate the strong desires of community participants. Through its programming, the Public Broadcasting Service's *Sesame Street,* for instance, has had a profound educational impact on children around the world. Creative use of video has long been a developmental and educational practice in Canada. One much-cited example in adult education is the Fogo Process of the 1960s, which was part of the Canadian National Film Board's (NFB) Challenge for Change series. (See also Chapter Eight, this volume.) The process used film as a way for rural Newfoundland residents to share their views on the importance of their way of life with the government and other Canadians. The NFB's Netsilik Eskimo film series is another innovative film project that was an authentic and collaborative re-creation of a precontact year in Arctic. The innovative American social studies curriculum MACOS (Man a Course of Study) from the 1970s used the Netsilik series to have elementary school students consider their own culture and the human condition. Giroux (1993) writes that educators seek to provide opportunities for learners to use their voices and add their narratives to the academic and educational landscape.

Video is an appropriate tool, and with the cost of cameras and computers falling, it is an educational bargain; video can provide the materials for bridging the gap of education and literacy for as many people as possible. Freire (1998) urges the colonized and disadvantaged to seize the tools of the dominant culture to drive their own development. The Fogo and Netsilik video projects were a success because participants were generous and used their voices to encourage others. Smith (1999) states that sharing views, ideas, and knowledge benefits the collective and creates a form of resistance. In each case, the video research project was a community effort and therefore was powerful in and of itself.

New Directions for Adult and Continuing Education • DOI: 10.1002/ace

To rationalize and understand literacy and education in the North, researchers and practitioners must reexamine what is happening and how it is happening, and work to create a new frame of reference that takes into account Aboriginal perspectives. It is vital for planners and practitioners in the North to move beyond Southern and Western systems of hierarchy and status. In this way, the issue can be addressed with solutions developed from a Northern viewpoint. Freire (1998) describes the oppressed students' situation as a "culture of silence" (p. 10), and hooks (1989) states that "moving from silence into speech is a revolutionary gesture . . . only as subjects can we speak. As objects, we remain voiceless—our beings defined and interpreted by others" (p. 12). Giroux (1988) proposes a "language of possibility" (p. 67) and urges educators "to provide the conditions for students to speak so that their narratives can be affirmed and engaged along with consistencies and contradictions that characterize such experiences" (1992, p. 205). Freire (1998) called it "naming their world" (pp. 75–76). Northern-produced projects can take back power, encourage dialogue, and dispel many of the myths that persist about the North and its people. The situation of Aboriginal Northerners is analogous to African American, Latino American, Native American, or any other racial, cultural, and socioeconomic minority population. It is unconscionable that educational inequality persists from the high Arctic tundra to the inner city.

The Video Research Process

The research had three parts: making the video, taking the video to the community for feedback, and recording the steps of the video-making process. Video is an accessible resource and archive to share research with a wider audience than is usually available through writing and reporting. Video can also capture nuance and visual meaning in a way that writing cannot.

This video-making process was very simple. Interviews about education and literacy were recorded and then edited using text screens to focus on specific themes related to lifelong learning, literacy, and family. We also obtained some archival footage that was used as cover, with participants' comments becoming voice-over. This simple process is easily duplicated and can readily flow out of research interviewing.

The video had fourteen participants (eleven female and three male) who were interviewed about education and literacy. Open-ended questions allowed them to share their stories and thoughts about education and literacy. Three focus groups (fifty-three participants in total) then watched the video and provided feedback on it, suggested other similar projects for the future, and gave suggestions for distribution in the community and region.

The first interview questions asked, "What is literacy and education?" and "Why is education important?" Then participants were asked more specific questions: "What is your history with education?" "Why is life long learning important?" and "Why is reading important?" Next, the interviewer

New Directions for Adult and Continuing Education • DOI: 10.1002/ace

asked, "How is family a big part of education?" The last two questions, "How are literacy and education important to the community and culture?" and "What is the importance of aboriginal language and traditional knowledge?" prompted personal and passionate responses. At the end of the interview, participants were asked if they had any final thoughts and messages for the community.

An appreciative inquiry (AI) method informed the video development process that included students and community members. The AI process benefits from video as it can be more readily captured and shared, especially over a large geographical region like the Western Arctic. By asking successful community members what they think and trying to get their message to the community, the research focused and built on positive experiences. No participants glossed over the difficulties they had experienced, but they chose to concentrate their messages on words of hope and encouragement. One video interview participant, a respected Inuvialuit leader and former premier, Nellie Cournoyea, expressed her hope for education with these words:

> Well, I believe that when we talk about education, we'll talk about all the education, and why is it good to the community. Education in terms of family well-being and family wellness is paramount. Education in self-discipline is paramount. And the overall academic higher learning is very important because it brings up the standards. If you're well educated, you are able to acquire more for your family, and you're able to be more confident in what you can do, like choices. And as well, you know, we can't forget the need for traditional and cultural knowledge and education. And those all have to be tied together. It's an overall need to make people strong and healthy and feel good about themselves.

Themes Arising from Research

In the video-making and interview process, responses focused around five main themes: Aboriginal history and knowledge valued, biculturalism, family and community, educational success, and increased prosperity through education. These themes were repeated by focus group participants, who not only gave feedback on the video but also answered the same questions as the video participants. The responses are combined here.

Aboriginal History and Knowledge Valued. The interviewees indicated that documenting oral history, traditional knowledge, and Aboriginal history is essential for understanding and supporting literacy and educational success in the North. Even more fundamental is the project of documenting the worldview and ways of knowing in the North. People need to have the words and opportunity to express their unique perspectives. The Northern perspective was expressed eloquently by video participant Liz Hansen, who defined *literacy* as "reading, writing, seeing, hearing. Just everything about life is literacy to me . . . even if you hear a bird singing, you know, that's literacy." The simplicity of her statement is not sentimental; rather, it is fundamental in linking the Aboriginal worldview to a unique way of knowing. Another video participant, Mabel English, shared her definition: "I think literacy is for everything. Where you learn. You learn how to handle your knife, your axe, you know, everything that's around that camp." Her definition is broad and completely embedded in her world. Mary Okheena, also a video participant, eloquently explained why this is so important:

> Traditional literacy means to me growing up; it makes me understand my parents and their culture, the way they think, the way they feel, the way things are changing now and to me it's really strong for me because if I lose my language and like you know the oral stories and what I hear from my elders . . . I lose the culture. It is all connected to me . . . . I know that traditional literacy and traditional language is really important for us to keep going. You can combine them both together and make it work, and you know it will really be kept alive. I find it when they are being taught at the start at the schools and in homes a lot of youth now, you know, when they see these things happening, the way the ancestors used to live and the way their language . . . they are really amazed how strong their ancestors were and how much skills they have and how much determination they had to do these, you know to make it on a day to day basis. . . . They find out their ancestors were really strong in many ways they didn't know.

Biculturalism. A second theme in the interviews and focus group process was biculturalism, best described by one workshop group participant who evoked the Tlicho (another First Nation group) motto, "Strong like two people." Video participants indicated that schools and institutions must work to be bicultural, and this must not be at the expense of the learners. Smith (1992) cautions that it is not a useful project if the energy put toward this bicultural process is made the responsibility of the Aboriginal people alone. Change must also come from the government and occur throughout the system. Not to make these changes is to perpetuate the status quo.

Family and Community. Another theme is the importance of the collective in the North. The Southern base unit is the individual, whereas the Northern base units are the family and the community. One focus group participant explains this continuum well: "Education is a great part of my life in order to gain good within the community, critical to my family to gain respect throughout the community . . . a prosperous life." There is no one to the exclusion of the other, but a continuum that privileges the group unit over the individual. Weaver (2000) expresses this concept succinctly: "I am We" (p. 227).

Participant Nellie Cournoyea explained the traditional Northern Aboriginal process of education and learning very clearly: "The importance of gaining knowledge was really being part of a group of people where you learnt by example." For the adult educator and society, this means all levels of education need to be valued—not just kindergarten to grade 12 or the increasingly popular early childhood education programs, but also adult education. Adult education needs to be a priority not only because more than half of all Aboriginal Northerners return to school as adults, but also because these adults are the caregivers, role models, breadwinners, and leaders for the next generation." Ever-practical single parent and successful adult student Cindy Voudrach asked viewers to be self-reliant because no one will do it for them. Parents' education is the most accurate indicator of educational success in children. Investing in adult education is also investing in families and children. This relationship needs to be made a priority for Northern education and funding. Adults are also the stewards of Northern culture, Northern tradition, and the Northern environment. This generation must be a priority and not ignored in favor of the next generation, as is too often the case. Funding children's programs looks good and feels good, but unless everyone is supported, the cycle will continue.

Educational Success. Southern education models and systems have had a relatively short and difficult genesis in the North. Maryann Ross, a video project participant, stated:

> Even now in this generation, they have to document the stories of my parents. How they made the transition from, you know, being on the land to being forced into residential schools, and the life they lived there, and how it impacted them, and it's indirectly impacted their children. And, you know, I also spent time in Grolier Hall [one of the Inuvik student hostels and part of the residential school system, where students are separated from their family and culture]. . . . But there was no negatives I can take from Grolier Hall because it was a good place for me. But, you know, there's a lot of other families that have been negatively impacted by the abuse that went on. The separation from their families, you know, feeling like they no longer belonged when they went home. So those are all the things that need to be—that story needs to be told. And we can't forget that, and we can't live that way again.

The most effective way to gauge educational success is to ask the learners, "What does success look like to you?" Several video participants and focus group participants described the shame family members felt about illiteracy, poor educational achievement, and residential schools. People have been judged by standards that are not their own, and this judgment has been painful and damaging, with devastating, lasting effects. Northerners need to be able to decide what is success for them, and educational institutions need to fully and appropriately support that success.

Increased Prosperity Through Education. The final theme is the conviction that education is essential. In both stages of the research, participants' employability and economic security were seen to be real and pressing concerns for all adult education students. A high school education is a bare minimum to cope in today's world. Video participant Cindy Voudrach is practical and succinct in stating her advice: "Stay in school. It is the best thing you can do for yourself. No one else is going to go out there and find a job for you and make money for you and you don't want to be stuck working for ten bucks an hour or whatever. You know it is hard. I mean you stick with school, you know you can do it. If I can do it anyone can do it."

Conclusion

All of the themes that rose out of this research can be a road map for how to work toward creating more equitable learning environments and opportunities. After the radical theories and great changes of the 1960s and 1970s, the revolution has stalled and in some cases backed up. Instead of becoming more flexible and responsive, education has become more rigid, with increased standardization and standardized testing, and it becomes even more rigid the more it is linked to employability. This trend shows no sign of abating as the demands for more and more education continue to rise.

Too often it is suggested that there is no interest or commitment to formal educational achievement by Northerners or any group that is not performing well in education. However, as video participants Erin Joe and Richard Baldwin candidly shared, "Education is important for our family. We want our child to get a good education. Just want her to be prepared for later in life so she won't have to struggle like we did. You know, we want her to have the things that we didn't have, and a good education will provide that."

According to this study, the will and desire are there. Video participants' and workshop participants' responses were unanimous on that issue. I can only conclude the problem is in the system. The system that is in place works only for some, and when that happens disproportionally to a specific group of people, the system must adapt. Innovation is the key. Video is not only a tool of representation, voice, and advocacy but also an important learning tool. It incorporates planning, editing, narrative construction, viewing, narrative analysis, and critique. The academic skills are the same as in traditional learning, but the method is different. Video participant Nellie Cournoyea confirms that responsiveness and adaptation are Northern cultural values:

> Education has always been important. Traditionally, education was—most people when they're talking about education they think about going to school or going to a hostel. Education is part of gaining knowledge to do what you have to do to survive. Traditionally, the type of knowledge you have to have was so critical just to survive or be a useful person. If you didn't have the skills that were taught on a daily basis—and that's education—but if you were not well educated in the skills that were required to survive, you couldn't be part of a functioning community. Traditionally, if you didn't, it was a matter of life and death.

Students and communities are waiting not for instructions or orders related to literacy and education but for engagement and dialogue. Video is a path toward communication; it can broaden the conversation and help keep it alive. It allows more ideas and voices to be shared and heard by more people. I have learned that any researcher concerned with practical reciprocity should consider video as a primary research tool. All that is needed are a camera, a microphone, and a computer. The research can come off the page and bear witness to learners' educational journeys.

References

Freire, P. *Pedagogy of the Oppressed.* (Rev. ed.) New York: Continuum, 1998.

Giroux, H. *Teachers as Intellectuals.* Westport, Conn.: Bergin and Garvey, 1988.

Giroux, H. "Literacy and the Politics of Difference." In C. Lankshear and P. L. MacLaren (eds.), *Politics, Praxis and the Postmodern.* Albany: State University of New York Press, 1993.

Government of the Northwest Territories, Education, Culture and Employment. *Towards Excellence 05: A report on Postsecondary Education in the NWT.* 2005. Retrieved March 16, 2008, from www.ece.gov.nt.ca/Divisions/ECE percent20Publications/towards percent20postsec percent20exc, 2005.

hooks, b. *Talking Back.* Boston: South End Press, 1989.

Organization for Economic Co-Operation and Development, and Statistics Canada. *Literacy in the Information Age.* Ottawa: Government of Canada, 2000.

Saku, J. C., and Bone, R. M. "Looking for Solutions in the Canadian North: Modern Treaties as a New Strategy." *Canadian Geographer,* 2000, *44*(3), 259–271.

Smith, G. H. "Education: Biculturalism or Separatism." In D. Novitz and B. Willmott (eds.), *New Zealand in Crisis.* Wellington, New Zealand: GP Books, 1992.

Smith, L. T. (1999). *Decolonizing Methodologies: Research and Indigenous Peoples.* London: Zed Books, 1999.

United Nations. "United Nations Declaration on the Rights of Indigenous Peoples." 2007. Retrieved February 7, 2008, from http://www.iwgia.org/sw248.asp, 2007.

Weaver, J. Indigenousness and Indigeneity. In Schwarz, H., and Sangeeta, R. (Eds.), *A companion to postcolonial studies* (pp. 221–235). Oxford: Blackwell Publishing Ltd, 2000.

SUZANNE ROBINSON is an adult educator at Inuvik Learning Centre, which is part of Aurora College's Aurora Campus in Inuvik Northwest Territories. She is also the president of the NWT Literacy Council.

3

This chapter describes four social movements that developed in the early twentieth century in Canada.

Social Change in Historical Perspective

Dorothy MacKeracher

Canada emerged as a nation through a confederation of provinces beginning in 1867. Since that time, responsibility for educational endeavors at all levels (elementary, secondary, and tertiary) has been assigned to the provincial governments, a responsibility they zealously guard. The federal government's role is to provide monies or transfer grants to the provinces, which decide how these funds will be spent. These decisions determine the shape of education within each province.

A range of educational endeavors, emerging as a result of various social movements, lies between the formal educational programs offered by publicly funded educational institutions and the vast array of informal learning activities conducted by individuals (Livingstone, 2005). The late nineteenth and early twentieth centuries provided fertile ground in which social movements were born in response to social and economic needs; developed and spread; and then became a stable organization with reliable funding, metamorphosed into a more flexible organization, or faded into history. The social movements that typify early Canadian adult education are many and varied, and in combination with the unique educational systems that emerged in each province, they gave rise to a patchwork quilt of adult education activities.

Trying to describe the beginnings and the full extent of this quilt is difficult. Where to begin? What social movements to include? How to assess the consequences of these social movements? Michael Welton (2006), a Canadian historian and adult educator, points out that at the start of the

NEW DIRECTIONS FOR ADULT AND CONTINUING EDUCATION, no. 124, Winter 2009 © 2009 Wiley Periodicals, Inc.
Published online in Wiley InterScience (www.interscience.wiley.com) • DOI: 10.1002/ace.350

twentieth century, major social movements were in place across Canada serving farmers, women, marginalized workers in remote campsites, young men and women drawn to urban centers to find work, and workers in organized unions.

In the nineteenth century, many Canadian social movements were imported from Great Britain or the United States: the Mechanics Institutes (precursors of public libraries and museums), the YMCA and YWCA, the Workers' Education Association, the cooperative movement, agricultural extension, and labor unions. This chapter briefly describes four social movements that evolved as Canadian endeavors in the early twentieth century: Frontier College, the Women's Institutes, the Antigonish movement, and the United Farmers of Canada (Saskatchewan). These social movements are still part of the ethos of Canadian adult education.

Social movements are described by Budd Hall (2006) as having four characteristics: informal interaction networks, shared beliefs and solidarity, collective action focusing on conflict, and the use of protest. He discusses the learning that evolves from and within social movements as affecting both individuals within the movement and those outside it who are influenced by its actions. This chapter first describes the four social movements and then discusses them in relation to these characteristics.

Frontier College

Frontier College, originally the Reading Camp Association, was developed by Alfred Fitzpatrick, a pastor from Pictou, Nova Scotia, who was concerned about the conditions under which unskilled manual laborers worked in remote camps associated with lumber and mining operations and road and railway building. Fitzpatrick's mission was to bring literacy skills and the social gospel to marginalized workers. He began in 1900 by setting up a reading room (actually a tent) in a lumber camp near his pastoral district in northern Ontario (Morrison, 1989). He hired a university student to oversee the reading room during the summer and to provide learning activities and Bible study to the workers when they had finished their day's work. By 1904, reading rooms existed in forty-two camps (Walter, 2003), and the new association was directed by Fitzpatrick and a board of volunteers.

In subsequent summers, Fitzpatrick arranged for students to be hired as laborers to work beside their coworkers during the day and provide Bible study, literacy training, educational discussions, and other activities in the evenings. This plan solved the problem of paying the laborer-teachers and changed the nature of the program. The laborer-teachers quickly discovered that focusing on the needs of the workers, rather than the needs of the social gospel movement, resulted in more relevant learning activities and better attendance (Morrison, 1989). From the beginning, the laborer-teachers gave Frontier College its unique characteristics.

New Directions for Adult and Continuing Education • DOI: 10.1002/ace

Fitzpatrick was joined in 1904 by Edwin Bradwin who assumed responsibility for supervising the work of laborer-teachers while Fitzpatrick expanded his efforts to muster public opinion and effect change in government policy. By 1918, most workers in the camps were recent immigrants who had fled the ravages of World War I and the Communist Revolution. The camps were perceived as potential hotbeds of communist thinking, so the laborer-teachers were charged with the task of Canadianizing the workers (Morrison, 1989). In 1919, Fitzpatrick wrote a learning resource to be used in the camps. The *Handbook for New Canadians* was a compilation of English language lessons, basic information about Canada, and advice on naturalization.

In 1920, Fitzpatrick published *University in Overalls: A Plea for Part-Time Study*. In it he addressed the lack of support by governments and educational institutions for continuing extension education for laborers and set out his ideas about how the entire industrial world could be converted into a university. He argued that "the great resources of nature should be used not to make the few rich, but to make the many wise" and urged educators to devise ways to take education to the workers: "We must go to them; they will not come to us" (Fitzpatrick, 1920, p. 72).

Fitzpatrick made a passionate plea to universities to establish extramural or part-time study. When his plea fell on deaf ears, he decided to establish Frontier College as an alternative to higher education. In 1922, the college was granted a dominion charter with degree-granting powers. However, education was a provincial responsibility, and Fitzpatrick could not convince any province or university to collaborate in the development of part-time study (Morrison, 1989), and the idea of a part-time university died with him in 1936. Frontier College and the laborer-teachers continued to serve laborers in remote settlements and camps under Bradwin's direction.

After World War II, the need for laborer-teachers diminished, and the number of remote camps for unskilled immigrant laborers declined. Frontier College responded to economic and social changes in society by forging "a new path, carving a role for itself in community development, technical programs, literacy training, and aid for the disenfranchised" (Frontier College, 2008). Today Frontier College continues to take education to marginalized men and women but has shifted its major attention to the needs of such persons in urban centers.

The Women's Institutes

In the late nineteenth century, Farmers' Institutes were organized to help farmers learn better farming and animal husbandry techniques. In 1897, the secretary of the Stoney Creek Farmers' Institute, Erland Lee, listened to Adelaide Hoodless deliver an address at the Ontario Agricultural College at Guelph on the importance of education for women. Hoodless asked the audience whether it was "of greater importance that a farmer should know more about the scientific care of his sheep and cattle, than that a farmer's wife should know how to care for her family" (MacDonald, 1986, p. 73). She wondered why the farmer should have labor-saving devices in his barn, while his wife toiled in their home without such benefits, often having to fetch water from the well to do her work (MacDonald, 1986).

Hoodless had lost her youngest child in 1889 to an intestinal ailment caused by drinking tainted milk. She had begun a crusade, through the Hamilton YWCA, to develop domestic science courses for young women to improve their housekeeping knowledge and skills. By 1897 she had moved on to badgering the Hamilton Board of Education and the Ontario Department of Education to offer such courses throughout the school system and encouraging the Agricultural College to offer teacher training courses in domestic science (MacDonald, 1986).

Lee asked Hoodless to speak to the wives of the members of his organization (MacDonald, 1986). In her address, Hoodless suggested that the women form their own organization and develop their own educational program. The suggestion was taken up, and a Women's Institute was born. At first the organization was purely social, but within a year, the women realized that they had a responsibility to educate themselves and to reach out and educate other women (Witter, 1979). By 1913, Women's Institutes had been established in most Canadian provinces. Their programs expanded to include personal growth opportunities, government lobbying, and health and community wellness initiatives (Federated Women's Institutes of Ontario, 2008).

During the 1930s, Women's Institutes adopted the study club methods encouraged by the Antigonish movement, and in the 1940s they included Farm Radio Forum study groups in their weekly programs (groups of people in rural Canada brought together to listen to a weekly half-hour program on farm issues, accompanied by study guides) (Witter, 1979). The institute became a "rural women's university. . . . . In many isolated communities, and on rural farms, the institute was the only organization where women could get together with other women to learn, grow and develop themselves by individual and group study and action" (p. 53).

The idea of the Women's Institute soon spread to Great Britain, where it received royal patronage. When introduced in 1917, the institute was set up to revitalize rural communities and encourage women to produce food during World War I; thus began a long association with jam making (Stamper, 1986). Women's Institutes soon spread and can be found today in over seventy countries; they are represented at the international level by the Associated Country Women of the World.

Although Hoodless had little to do with organizing and developing the Women's Institutes beyond her initial involvement, she is usually cited as one of the founders. Today she is criticized for not joining the women's suffrage movement. She played a prominent role in the development of the Victorian

Order of Nurses, an organization dedicated to providing home care for recovering patients, and the National Council of Women, an organization concerned with the overall well-being of women in Canada (MacDonald, 1986). Her position on the vote for women therefore seems paradoxical given that she spent almost all of her time urging women to change the conditions under which they were living and to become better educated on all matters that concerned their well-being.

The Antigonish Movement

The Antigonish movement grew out of the wretched economic and social conditions following World War I that affected farming, mining, and fishing communities in eastern Nova Scotia. The man who took up the cause was Father James Tompkins, a Catholic priest who believed that people could learn to help themselves. In 1913, Father Jimmy was vice president of Saint Francis Xavier University, a small Catholic university in Antigonish, Nova Scotia. He attended a meeting in London, England, where he encountered the ideas of the socialist movement of adult education and returned with the belief that "by teaching adults, universities would spark economic growth and improve the lives of people and communities" (Lotz and Welton, 1997, p. 25). He urged Saint Francis to establish an extension department that would educate the common people and provide a useful education to help them rebuild their lives. The university rejected the idea. He then took his campaign to the public through local newspapers in an attempt to persuade the university to change its mind. He consolidated his ideas in a pamphlet, *Knowledge for the People*, and organized a People's School with other professors at Saint Francis. The school's purpose was to demonstrate the need for "adult education combining spiritual and practical works of mercy" (p. 73) and to teach people by giving them the tools to improve their lives and communities. He did not teach any subjects himself but occasionally lectured on his favorite formula illustrating social progress (Laidlaw, 1961, p. 64):

$$\text{People} \times \text{resources} \times \text{education} = \text{Progress.}$$

In 1922, Father Jimmy pushed church authorities too far when he supported a campaign to form an integrated, nondenominational university for the Maritime provinces, and he soon found himself the pastor of a church in Canso, a small, destitute fishing village in eastern Nova Scotia. His ideas, however, had greatly influenced his cousin, Moses Michael Coady, also a Catholic priest and a faculty member of Saint Francis. Coady took over the task of prodding the university to form an extension department. Father Jimmy has been described as "an extremely abrasive individual, forever prodding people to read a book, discuss a pamphlet, take some action. . . . He did not do things for people"; however, he would suggest how they might solve problems and provided some of the resources they might need (Lotz and Welton, 1987, p. 103). Coady has been described as a charismatic man, an impressive public speaker who projected "a transcendental vision of the good life" (p. 104) that could result from extension education.

At Canso, Father Jimmy helped the people to get a road built, lent the fishermen money to build their own lobster canning plant, and encouraged the community to renew itself through its own efforts (Lotz and Welton, 1987). In 1927, the Canso fishermen, at the urging of Father Jimmy, drew up resolutions to be forwarded to the MacLean Royal Commission, then investigating the fisheries in the Maritime provinces. The commission concluded that the adoption of "adult education for the whole of Canada and particularly for the Maritime Provinces" (Lotz and Welton, 1997, p. 90) was the best solution to economic despair. In 1928, Saint Francis set up the Extension Department and appointed Coady its first director.

The work of the Extension Department focused on the establishment of study clubs, cooperatives, credit unions, guilds, and settlement housing (Alexander, 1997). Study clubs were formed when local people gathered in kitchens and parlors, church halls and general stores, to discuss matters of importance to them. Facilitators were hired to provide assistance to these groups and unite those who wanted to learn with those who had knowledge and skills to share. The department provided study materials and resources, which were distributed through the mail.

Coady was joined in these endeavors by Angus "A.B." MacDonald, who assumed responsibility for helping communities develop cooperatives and credit unions and for publishing a newsletter for cooperators. In 1930 Coady enlisted the aid of the Sisters of St. Martha to provide assistance. Two sisters took up the challenge. Since they received no pay, they were a godsend to a university department that was always short of funds. Sister Marie Michael MacKinnon oversaw the lending library and prepared materials for the study clubs. Sister Irene Doyle, another cousin of Coady, took charge of the handicraft program, helping women learn skills and form marketing cooperatives for their products (Casey, 2001).

The work of the Extension Department spread throughout the three Maritime provinces. By 1938, there were 350 clubs composed entirely of women (Delaney, 1985) and over 2,000 mixed clubs for both men and women (Lotz and Welton, 1987). The handicraft program quickly expanded beyond the financial limitations of the Extension Department. In 1942, at a province-wide conference, Sister Irene recommended that the provincial government assume responsibility for encouraging and promoting the cottage industries spawned by the handicraft program, and the Division of Handicrafts was established in the Department of Industry (Casey, 2001).

The Antigonish movement presented itself to the world as the middle way between the extremities of collectivism and individualism. The movement could also be described as a third way on the Canadian left: a radical social tradition in its own right that differed from social democracy and communism (Lotz and Welton, 1987). The study clubs continued unabated until World War II, when declining interest accompanied improving economic conditions. The Extension Department continued to encourage and support the development of cooperatives as long as members were interested (Welton, 2001).

In 1960, the work of the Extension Department was expanded to include overseas work through the Coady International Institute. Today the institute trains workers from developing countries and focuses its programs on asset-based community development, microfinance, peace building, community-based resource management, advocacy, and the development of knowledge networks (Plumb and McGray, 2006). (For further discussion of the Antigonish movement, see Chapter Eight, this volume.)

The United Farmers of Canada (Saskatchewan)

In the late nineteenth century, farmers organized into a variety of cooperative ventures to improve their agricultural techniques and market their produce at the best possible price. In 1900, the Territorial Grain Grower's Association was formed to serve the needs of a growing population of farmers moving into the western territories (later the provinces of Saskatchewan and Alberta) and to respond to growing agitation over the refusal of the Canadian Pacific Railway to allow farmers to load grain directly into railcars (Canadian Encyclopedia, 2008). Farmers were forced to sell their grain to elevator operators at unfavorable prices. In 1900, federal government legislation changed the regulations to favor the farmers: a farmer or group of farmers could load grain directly into railcars provided they had enough grain to fill the car. The railroad paid no attention to the legislation and refused to provide railcars. The Grain Growers' Association sued the railway and won, thereby energizing the existing agrarian movement and establishing itself as an influential farmers' organization (Stutt, 1950).

Agrarian reform organizations were formed originally as a response to specific grievances in buying and selling commodities. Prairie farmers, despite racial, linguistic, and religious differences, shared a common suspicion of big business and urban interests. However, their organizations vacillated between concerns for the economic welfare of individual farmers and the collective need to take political action. In 1905, the Territorial Association was divided into the Saskatchewan Grain Growers' Association (SGGA) and the Alberta Farmers' Association. Little agreement existed within these associations about which side of the political spectrum should be supported. Farmers' associations formed and re-formed themselves under a variety of names, combining with other organizations to spawn, throughout the mid-twentieth century, new political parties that challenged the traditional two-party system of eastern Canada (Canadian Encyclopedia, 2008).

In 1924, the SGGA formed the Saskatchewan Wheat Pool as a cooperative venture. Field men were hired by the provincial government to coordinate educational activities, which included picnics and rallies, conventions and meetings, study groups, farm forums, and cooperative schools. The field men collaborated with the Extension Department of the University of Saskatchewan and the Adult Education Division of the Saskatchewan Department of Education (Stutt, 1950).

In 1926, the SGGA combined with the more radical Farmers' Union of Canada to form the United Farmers of Canada, Saskatchewan Section (UFC). In the 1930s, the organization was dominated by radicals who favored political action. They developed a socialist platform and, in cooperation with the Independent Labour party, formed the Cooperative Commonwealth Federation (CCF). The CCF gained political power in Saskatchewan in 1944 and was the first social democratic party elected to power in North America (Canadian Encyclopedia, 2008).

In 1910, Violet and Jack McNaughton became active members of the SGGA. Violet immediately immersed herself in the work of the organization. She was, with her husband's support, an adamant agrarian feminist (Taylor, 2000). At the 1913 SGGA convention, she helped establish the Women's Grain Growers (WGG) Association and became its first president. Through the WGG, she began a crusade to have trained midwives, more nurses, and affordable doctors and hospitals in close proximity to all farm families (Steer, 1979). Her efforts spurred the province to pass legislation in 1916 for the founding of union hospitals and the hiring of municipal doctors and nurses. Her unrelenting advocacy for better medical care for farm families led to universal medical care in Saskatchewan, introduced in 1944 by the newly elected CCF government, and eventually in Canada (introduced in 1962) (Library and Archives Canada, 2008; Steer, 1979; Taylor, 2000).

The WGG's activities were rooted in the life of the farm family and the belief that the work of farm women was necessary for the nation; therefore, they should have a voice in the nation's business and should be able to live well (Taylor, 2000). Violet McNaughton worked as an organizer and adult educator in Saskatchewan for nearly fifty years. In the 1910s and 1920s, she focused on direct organizational and educational work in the belief that such actions could lead to a new social order. Steer (1979) describes McNaughton's educational beliefs as being based on cooperation rather than competition. Men and women would work together, each group bringing to the endeavor unique viewpoints. Before they could work together, though, they had to become aware of the important issues influencing their lives and understand their individual responsibilities in relation to these issues. Then, in small community groups, people would make decisions for action based on their awareness and understanding; finally, they would act to improve their own lives as well as the lives of others. McNaughton believed that "knowledge used in this way, equalled power" (Steer, 1979, p. 44).

McNaughton described how a local SGGA study group could be formed when one interested person talked to friends and neighbors. These active, involved, committed individuals would then bring in more individuals to form a district association, which would elect executive officers and plan future programs. Finally the district group would affiliate with the provincial association, send delegates to conventions, and form a women's auxiliary. Steer (1979) reports that McNaughton believed that "it was the individual's responsibility to become more articulate so that the common sense of the many and not the brilliance of the few would determine the direction of the organization" (p. 51).

McNaughton became disillusioned in the late 1920s when prohibition was exchanged for government control of liquor outlets, women's suffrage did not result in the reconstruction of Canadian society, and efforts to deliver social justice were diverted toward the establishment of provincial government social services (Steer, 1979). In the growing malaise of the 1930s, McNaughton turned to educating farm families indirectly through her writings for the *Western Producer*, a publication of the Wheat Board, which boasted of having a feature for every member of the family (University of Saskatchewan Archives, 2008). Even as a journalist, McNaughton believed in the use of interactive discussion for educational purposes. She would write a short piece on a controversial topic and then welcome, print, and comment on the responses, including those that disagreed with her position (Steer, 1979).

Conclusion

The social movements described in this chapter conform, more or less, with the characteristics that Hall (2006) outlined. All offered informal interaction networks through the use of small study groups. All were grounded in shared beliefs and solidarity. All were concerned with taking collective action to improve the conditions under which individuals and communities existed. Their focus on conflict varied from responses to individual problems in Frontier College to political responses to varied problems in the WGG and later the United Farmers of Canada (Saskatchewan Section). The use of protest did not seem to be part of the activities of Frontier College or the Women's Institutes, but they did form part of the activities in the Antigonish movement and the UFC.

Learning within the movement was a primary concern in all four organizations, although the Women's Institutes began with concerns for the social well-being of members. The most interesting characteristic of these social movements was the learning they spawned among outside groups and individuals. Frontier College, which raised concerns among outsiders about adult literacy, still provides a voice for marginalized men and women whose lack of literacy and numeracy skills leaves them ill equipped to participate fully in the Canadian economy. Where laborer-teachers were once sent to mining and logging camps in remote areas, they are now sent into the streets of urban centers.

The Women's Institutes raised awareness of the benefits of educating not just rural women but all women throughout the world. The Antigonish movement strongly encouraged the use of small study groups and cooperatives to help local communities raise their standard of living, a conviction that was later adopted worldwide by groups concerned about social change and community improvement. The United Farmers of Canada (Saskatchewan Section) and its women's auxiliaries helped change public policies that affected and continue to affect the lives of Canadian men and women in relation to their access to health care.

References

Alexander, A. *The Antigonish Movement*. Toronto: Thompson Educational Publishing, 1997.

Canadian Encyclopedia. "United Farmers of Canada." Retrieved October 10, 2008, from www.thecanadianencyclopedia.com.

Casey, K. "The Antigonish Movement: Her Story." Unpublished master's thesis, University of New Brunswick, 2001.

Delaney, I. *By Their Own Hands: A Fieldworker's Account of the Antigonish Movement*. Hantsport, N.S.: Lancelot Press, 1985.

Federated Women's Institutes of Ontario. "About FWIO." Retrieved October 10, 2008, from www.fwio.on.ca/Contribute/about/about.asp.

Fitzpatrick, A. *Handbook for New Canadians*. Toronto: Ryerson Press, 1919.

Fitzpatrick, A. *University in Overalls: A Plea for Part-Time Study*. Toronto: Hunter-Rose Co., 1920.

Frontier College. "About Frontier College." Retrieved October 10, 2008, from www.frontiercollege.ca.

Hall, B. L. "Social Movement Learning: Theorizing a Canadian Tradition." In T. Fenwick, T. Nesbit, and B. Spencer (eds.), *Contexts of Adult Education: Canadian Perspectives*. Toronto: Thompson Educational Publishing, 2006.

Laidlaw, A. F. *The Campus and the Community: The Global Impact of the Antigonish Movement*. Montreal: Harvest House Limited, 1961.

Library and Archives Canada. "Violet McNaughton. Celebrating Women's Achievements." Retrieved October 10, 2008, from www.collectionscanada.gc.ca/femmes/002026–5013-e.html.

Livingstone, D. W. "Basic findings of the 2004 Canadian Learning and Work Survey." Paper presented at the Future of Lifelong Learning and Work Conference, Toronto, June 20, 2005. Retrieved October 10, 2008, from lifelong.oise.utoronto.ca/papers/WALLBasicSummJune05.pdf.

Lotz, J., and Welton, M. R. "'Knowledge for the People': The Origins and Development of the Antigonish Movement." In M. R. Welton (ed.), *Knowledge for the People: The Struggle for Adult Learning in English-speaking Canada, 1828–1973*. Toronto: OISE Press, 1987.

Lotz, J., and Welton, M. R. *Father Jimmy: The Life and Times of Jimmy Tompkins*. Wreck Cove, NS: Breton Books, 1997.

MacDonald, C. *Adelaide Hoodless: Domestic crusader*. Toronto: Dundurn Press, 1986.

Morrison, J. H. *Camps and Classrooms: A Pictorial History of Frontier College*. Toronto: Frontier College Press, 1989.

Plumb, D., and McGray, R. *Learning Communities: CCL Review of the State of the Field in Adult Learning*. Halifax, NS: Mount St. Vincent University, 2006.

Stamper, A. "Education and the Women's Institutes." *Adult Education*, 1986, 59(1), 33–38.

Steer, S. L. "The Beliefs of Violet McNaughton: Adult Educator, 1909–1929." Unpublished master's thesis, University of Saskatchewan, 1979.

Stutt, R. L. "The Saskatchewan Wheat Pool and Education." In J. R. Kidd (ed.), *Adult Education in Canada*. Toronto: Garden City Press Co-operative, 1950.

Taylor, G. M. "Let Us Co-Operate: Violet McNaughton and the Co-Operative Ideal." In B. Fairbairn and I. MacPherson (eds.), *Co-Operatives in the Year 2000: Memory, Mutual Aid, and the Millennium*. Saskatoon: University of Saskatchewan, Centre for the Study of Co-operatives, 2000.

University of Saskatchewan Archives. "The Western Producer." Retrieved October 10, 2008, from scaa.usask.ca/gallery/wheatpool/en_ventures-western.php.

Walter, P. "Literacy, Imagined Nations, and Imperialism: Frontier College and the Construction of British Canada, 1899–1933." *Adult Education Quarterly*, 2003, 54(1), 42–58.

Welton, M. R. "Intimations of a Just Learning Society: From the United Farmers of Alberta to Henson's Provincial Plan in Nova Scotia." In T. Fenwick, T. Nesbit, and B. Spencer (eds.), *Contexts of Adult Education: Canadian Perspectives*. Toronto: Thompson Educational Publishing, 2006.

Welton, M. R. "History of Adult Education—Why?" In T. Barer-Stein and M. Kompf (eds.), *The Craft of Teaching Adults*. (3rd ed.) Toronto: Irwin Publishing, 2001.

Witter, S. "An Historical Study of Adult Education in Two Canadian Women's Organizations: The Federated Women's Institutes of Canada and the Young Women's Christian Association of Canada, 1870–1978." Unpublished master's thesis, University of British Columbia, 1979.

DOROTHY MACKERACHER *is professor emerita for adult education on the Faculty of Education, University of New Brunswick, Fredericton, Canada.*

New Directions for Adult and Continuing Education • DOI: 10.1002/ace

4

Drawing on an analysis of official policies and initiatives, this chapter presents the specific situation of adult education in Quebec, its problems, and the solutions that have been devised.

Perspectives on Adult Education in Quebec

Mohamed Hrimech

Canada is an officially bilingual (English and French) country, but for the most part, English and French people live in different areas of the country. Quebec's official language is French, although it has a large English-speaking community, especially in Montreal. The United States does not have an official second language, but adult education practitioners regularly work with learners whose first language is not English and in communities where other languages are spoken. The Quebec situation is unique in North America: French is a minority language, considered to be endangered in Canada, and education and culture play a central role in its preservation.

Due to specific historical and political factors, adult educators in Quebec face different challenges from practitioners in other parts of the country or in the United States. These challenges can be considered threefold: preservation of the French language, educating the workforce, and integrating new immigrants. This chapter presents the specific situation and problems of adult education in Quebec, as well as the solutions that have been devised. For this purpose, I draw mostly on analysis of governmental or official policies and orientations about the present and future of adult education. I put forward that adult educators, their training and recognition, are the missing link between the objectives and achievements of adult education in Quebec. This gap has been rarely addressed, if at all.

NEW DIRECTIONS FOR ADULT AND CONTINUING EDUCATION, no. 124, Winter 2009 © 2009 Wiley Periodicals, Inc.
Published online in Wiley InterScience (www.interscience.wiley.com) • DOI: 10.1002/ace.351

Adult and Continuing Education in Quebec

The rate of participation in adult education in Canada (34 percent) is situated in the midrange of member countries of the Organization for Economic Co-Operation and Development (OECD) (Tuijman and Boudard, 2001). Most of this participation is for professional reasons. In Canada, according to the OECD, only 60 percent of the population reaches what is considered the minimum competency level in reading and mathematics. In today's knowledge society, information and communication technologies play a pivotal role. Market globalization, the complexities of job duties, and the need for constant innovation to stay competitive in the global market make continuing education necessary for adapting to change in the workplace and to fully participate in society (Ministère de l'éducation du Québec, 2000).

In its 2002 review of adult learning, the OECD identified a significant lack of coordination in adult learning programs in Canada. This gap occurs between federal and provincial governments, as well as between the public and private sectors. The OECD also identified the absence of a national forum for adult learning as a major barrier to developing adult learning initiatives that are coherent, consistent, effective, and universally available. The Adult Learning Knowledge Centre was created to address these gaps and to become a national reference point and key resource for Canada's adult learning activities (it was closed in 2009 mostly for financial reasons and to my knowledge, the work has not been taken up by others. In Quebec, Inchauspé (1999) presented a tentative policy of continuing education based on an exhaustive analysis of the situation.

In Quebec, an average of 18 percent of the population fifteen years of age and older has fewer than nine years of schooling (Bélanger, 2002). The gap between all of Canada and Quebec regarding enrollment in adult education was 1 percent in 1984, but by 1997 it had increased to 7 percent. There was a sharp drop in enrollment in Quebec: 27 percent in 1991 and 21 percent in 1997. These years correspond to major and persistent government budget cuts in funding for adult education. Programs were also closed in universities.

For decades, Quebec's French population had limited access to education beyond the primary level and was far behind the English population in education, science, and business. The "quiet revolution" in the 1960s was a rejection of traditionalism, conservatism, and the religious values that distinguished Quebec Catholic society. This period of Quebec history was characterized by a rapid modernization and intense social change through educational, political, and economic venues. These changes had great impact on the educational level of Quebecers. The "Royal Commission of Inquiry on Education in the Province of Quebec" produced a five-volume report known as the "Parent Report." In this report, education was no longer considered a luxury but a right, and most of the recommendations put forward were implemented by the liberal government. The report triggered extensive reforms; giant steps have been achieved in education, and the number of Quebecers attending postsecondary or higher education has never been so high. Still, these successes are relative; much remains to be done in many areas, for example, reducing the dropout rate, particularly among boys and immigrants. Special efforts need to be made, especially in adult education and continuing education. The Quebec government is aware of this situation and has devised policies and plans to address these problems (Conseil supérieur de l'éducation, 2003; Inchauspé, 1999). Today's knowledge economy and the emerging educational societies necessitate that a substantial proportion of the workforce be highly educated. Without a secondary school diploma or diploma of vocational studies, it is becoming hard to find a minimally interesting job and join the productive workforce. This situation is exacerbated by the fact that the workforce is aging as baby boomers begin to enter retirement in massive numbers. Also, many adult immigrants attracted to the province need to learn French or need additional training to join the workforce.

Quebec can be characterized as a province that has a large deficit in basic education, especially among its workforce. This has negative consequences for the performance of organizations, though recent results show improvement, especially since the recent reform of education (Ministère de l'éducation du Québec, 2000). Basic education is necessary for successful social and economic integration into society and is the basis for future development and lifelong learning (Ministère de l'éducation du Québec, 2002a). Quebec's education system is achieving encouraging results in comparison to other similar countries of the OECD. However, it still has one of the highest provincial rates of illiteracy in Canada. An estimated 1.5 million Quebecers have difficulty reading, writing, and using texts and math in work or everyday life. In addition, "Boys account for two thirds of students experiencing dropout academic delays and the majority of students leaving without diploma" (Ministère de l'éducation du Québec, 2000, p. 8). This situation has a direct impact on adults' employability, life conditions, and participation in society (Statistiques Canada, 2007). Statistics Canada estimates that more than 1.5 million Quebecers aged fifteen to sixty-four do not have a diploma. In 2001, some 230,000 adults were enrolled in general and professional education, which means that a large number of those who did not get a sufficient basic education were on their way to correcting the situation (Ministère de l'éducation du Québec, 2002a). Adult education is expected to compensate for the shortcomings of the basic educational system.

The Role and Importance of Adult Education

In Canada, participation in adult education is around 30 percent of the population. In northern European countries like Germany and Sweden, participation levels are above 50 percent (Bélanger, 2002). In contrast, the participation of adults in educational activities in Quebec steadily decreased between 1991 and 1997, from 27.5 percent to 20.6 percent. But more recently, the number of adults who register in complementary or compensatory education has been growing again. This growth is mostly due to young people returning to adult education evening courses to get their secondary school diploma or in professional training or people who register in nonformal education, for example in evening classes where they learn new skills without seeking formal recognition or accreditation by an institution. Nonformal education is also called community education and refers to learning and training which takes place outside recognized educational institutions. Also, many of them use informal education or self-directed learning to improve their job-related competencies (Bélanger, 2002; Livingstone, 1999). Informal learning or education refers to the acquisition of new skills and knowledge through self-initiated activities, such as reading, that take place mainly outside formal educational institutions such as schools. Self-directed or informal learning has drawn a lot of attention and research in both Europe and in North America. It is widespread and can complement formal and nonformal education and training skills; development and renewal has not been stressed enough. A clear strategy of prior learning recognition and the development of procedures to assess this type of learning should increase its use and may bring some interest and respect to the field. Otherwise, the skills learned through work and life experience will not be encouraged and will remain unaccounted for.

In 2002, the first governmental policy on adult and continuing education was put forward, along with an action plan and funding of $450 million Canadian dollars (Bélanger, 2002; Ministère de l'éducation du Québec, 2002b). This policy and the action plan are tailored to the needs and reality of adults. The main goals of the policy were to secure an initial basic education for the highest possible number of people, maintaining and improving the competency level of adults, valuing and recognizing their prior learning and competencies (prior learning validation), removing obstacles to accessibility to education, and promoting perseverance in education. As a result of this policy, thirty-three thousand more adults enrolled in adult education every year since the policy went into effect. It aimed also at promoting continuing education, the enhancement of reception and reference services (*Services d' accueil et de reference*) in adult education centers, the development of evaluation tools for the recognition of prior learning and competencies, and the establishment of loans for part-time education. The reception and reference services are set up to receive and give information, counselling, and guidance to adults pertaining to learning projects that are related to their work. The plan sets out more than thirty steps to translate the policy's four goals into practice, among them the prevention of and fight against dropout and illiteracy. Basic education for the greatest number is the first challenge of adult and continuing education in Quebec. Supporting Quebecers in their continuing education efforts and encouraging participation and persistence are among the challenges facing the education system.

New Directions for Adult and Continuing Education • DOI: 10.1002/ace

The training of specialist researchers and practitioners in adult education has dropped to almost zero in Quebec during the past decade. The training of teachers and other practitioners in primary and secondary schools is administered by strict rules that control entry to the profession. By contrast, adult education is not regulated by the state, and there are no standards for entry into the field or for professional development. For this reason, adult educators have been recruited among all other professionals without any formal training in adult education theory or methods. The departments of adult education in most Quebec universities are either nonexistent or have shrunk to the point that they contain no more than two or three faculty. The survival of some of these departments is constantly threatened. Research has suffered as well from a persistent lack of funding. This situation is somewhat surprising since adult education in other provinces seems to be vigorous and healthy, and the government seems well aware that the ongoing renewal of skills is a basic requirement for adults in an information society.

Preservation of the French Language. Each civilization is supported by a language, and all languages contribute to the development of humanity and carry culture and values. The French language in North America has had this mission for the past four hundred years. Today for Quebecers, French is "a constituent element of their nationality, a condition for the survival of a society attached to its values and its faith, and the 'living environment' and the critical element for the progress of an entire people and even an entire society" (Conseil supérieur de la langue française, 2007 p. 9). It has become the symbol of Quebec identity and a collective reference in a multicultural society and an integrated global economy (Stefanescu and Georgeault, 2005). The status of language, its official place and actual situation in society, is considered essential to its survival (Béland, 2008). In the past forty years, the situation of the French language has greatly improved; Francophones now work mostly in their language and earn equivalent salaries as Anglophone citizens.

The Charter of the French Language, also known as Bill 101, is the law passed in 1977 which defined French as the language of the majority of the population and the official language of Quebec. It framed fundamental rights for everyone in the province and aimed to make French the everyday language of work, instruction, communication, commerce, and business. This law, once criticized and challenged in courts, has been fundamental to the revival and progress of the French language in the workplace and in schools. For example, children of immigrants are required to go to French-speaking schools. Through an unprecedented mobilization, artists and writers fought vehemently for the place the language enjoys today in business, art, and science. The survival of the French language and culture is considered to be threatened from the outside and from inside society. It is threatened from the outside by the dominance of the English language in culture, science, economy, and finance, especially for the 6 million Francophones in a predominantly English-speaking North America.

The new technologies of mass communication, television, and the Internet have added to the dominance and power of English. The popularity of many American television series in Canada is eloquent testimony to this phenomenon. These technologies influence linguistic transfers (speaking at home another language than the native language) among young people, both immigrants and native French speakers. From within, immigration is considered as endangering the survival and development of the French language in Quebec. French is used in work and in institutions, but the language spoken in the home may be something other than English or French. Because English has been the language of science, technology, and business for a long time, it is not surprising that linguistic transfers are mostly from French to English or from other languages to English or French. English exerts an enormous power, mainly on newly educated generations and immigrants. In the workplace, regulation makes the use of French compulsory, so Francophones can work in their language. Nevertheless, English is widely used in many organizations. Generally speaking, Bill 101 adopted in the seventies requires immigrant children to attend French schools. Although this legislation has been criticized and challenged many times in court, it has been quite successful. It has regenerated the French language and helped open French schools to immigrant children who used to go mainly to English schools. In addition, the right of the Quebec government to select which immigrants are permitted to settle in the province has helped the French language. Knowledge of the French language is an important selection criterion for people who choose to settle in the province. For others, *francisation* (an orientation to French culture and language) of Quebec society necessitates teaching the French language to thousands of adult immigrants. Evening schools and specialized centers created for this purpose have had some success. Adult educators have contributed to this effort, but budgets for teaching French to immigrants have been reduced recently; some centers have closed and the government has come up with new plans for funding the teaching of French to immigrants.

"Working in French" has become a motto for those who consider the French language in danger and seek to protect it. The use of French remains fragile, and many new challenges have surfaced—the weight of Anglophone immigration one of them.

Integrating New Immigrants. Integration of new immigrants and the preservation of the French language have become tightly linked in a context of an aging Francophone population and the growing number of immigrants from nonFrancophone countries. In the past twenty years, Quebec has received more than 722,000 immigrants—about 16.5 percent of those who arrived in Canada. The Quebec government plans to raise the number of immigrants admitted from forty-five thousand a year to fifty-five thousand by 2010. More than 84 percent of those who arrived between 2002 and

2006 declared a native language other than English or French (Institut de la statistique du Québec, 2008). Most immigrants (85 percent) choose to live in the Montreal area. About 40 percent of those admitted in recent years do not speak French. According to the Conseil supérieur de la langue française (2008), a Quebec institution devoted to the defense and preservation of the French language, there needs to be a massive investment in the *francisation* of immigrants, especially since only about 15 percent of those from Anglophone or Anglophile countries, once in the province, choose to learn, speak, and use French at work (Conseil supérieur de l'éducation, 2007). Immigrants who are not from Latin or Francophone countries have been impermeable to all measures of *francisation* for the past thirty years. Immigrants who choose Quebec choose also to live in Montreal and its suburbs, which in 2006 had, respectively, 20.6 percent and 13.4 percent of Anglophones. From 1991 to 2006, the percentage of those who speak French at home fell from 57.4 to 54.2 percent, while those who speak English remained about the same (26.0 percent and 25.2 percent) and those who speak another language rose from 16.6 percent to 20.6 percent. The decrease in the number of Francophones comes mostly from the rise of the number of Anglophones. "Immigration is an important element because it changes the linguistic composition of the population and the accumulated linguistic capital" (Béland, 2008, p. 7). Most immigrants have to choose between French and English for work and public activities, a choice that influences what language they speak in private and, consequently, the native language of the second generation (Béland, 2008). Millions of dollars must be invested in the *francisation* of immigrants in the coming years, and the government wants them to learn French in greater numbers and do it earlier and more successfully.

The most important issues for immigrants are learning the French language to join the labor force and the recognition of diplomas and prior learning from their countries of origin. In Quebec, forty-five occupations, including physician, nurse, lawyer, and engineer, are subject to control by their respective professional associations. The Office des professions du Québec and forty-five professional groups act as watchdogs to limit tightly the entry of immigrants who hold diplomas from foreign universities, effectively shutting them out from the professions. For example, although Quebec has a shortage of doctors in some specialties and in many regions of the province, foreign-trained doctors have tremendous difficulty in having their credentials recognized so they can work in their field. This situation has caused much frustration among the most qualified immigrants, pushing them back to their countries of origin, other provinces, or the United States.

The rate of employment is higher among immigrants, especially the young ones from certain ethnic or cultural origins often named "visible minorities." Lack of qualification is not the only explanation for this situation. In fact, many immigrants work in jobs for which they are highly overqualified. Visible minorities are still underrepresented in public service, government, and well-paid jobs generally. Some progress has been achieved in some fields like education, but a great deal remains to be done.

The Office québécois de la langue française (2008) analyzed data from the 2006 population survey on language and immigration and concluded that Quebec needs to build its future on French as a common language, but it also recommends that it not fear assimilation due to ethnic and linguistic diversity. French language in Quebec is a minority language in North America and Canada, and is too precarious to develop without state support. The low birth rate of the French-speaking population and the increasing importance of Anglophone immigrants may change the linguistic balance or situation. The French language may become less used by new immigrants and even by native French speakers due to "linguistic transfer" mostly to English. In other words, the report reveals tensions and fears that the French language may lose ground (Conseil supérieur de la langue française, 2007, 2008). The Bouchard-Taylor report (2008) makes the same point and notes the complex task of integrating immigrants from more than one hundred countries into French society while respecting their original cultures and beliefs. Their participation in and adherence to a democratic society and its fundamental values and their participation in a public common culture must also be ensured. Creating the right conditions for learning French is thus creating the conditions for a better understanding of the Quebec society and its culture.

Educating the Workforce. School and work are tightly linked socializing institutions for both native people and immigrants. Successful integration and francisation of immigrants can be completed only in the workplace. Even after their training and entry into the labor force, workers have to continue learning to maintain their competency level and help their organizations maintain a competitive edge (Ministère de l'éducation du Québec, 2000z). The aging of the population and the drop in birthrate make it more difficult to renew the labor force in Quebec (Ministère de l'emploi et de la solidarité sociale, 2003). Maintaining and enhancing the competencies of working people is vital for economic growth and social development.

Until the early 1990s, there was a lack of employer investment in the education and training of the workforce, which prompted government action. Bill 90, the law for the development and training of the labor force, has had a great impact on the development of adult professional education and training in organizations (Bélanger and Robitaille, 2008). The "1 percent" law, as it is sometimes called, was adopted in 1995 to help develop adult professional education and training in organizations. This law was modified in 2007 to become "the law for the development and reconnaissance competencies of labour force," referred to generally as the "law on competencies." According to this law, organizations that spend more than $1 million annually on salaries must invest 1 percent of that amount on training their personnel. Employers who do not invest 1 percent in training must deposit the equivalent amount in a fund to finance annual grants for projects dedicated to competency development. This law has given tremendous momentum to the offering of and demand for professional education in the province, though it has been criticized. One issue has been that some small organizations have paid as much as large organizations but gained less, since some of their funds were pooled to pay for the education of employees in larger organizations.

As well, although there are some loose regulations about the qualifications of trainers and firms specializing in training the workforce, there have been some complaints about irrelevant course content and inappropriate training methods. Nevertheless, there are some safeguards. The Order of Chartered Human Resources and Industrial Relations Advisors of Quebec is devoted mainly to improving the quality of professional practice through the professional development and accreditation of affiliated members. It counts many trainers and providers.

The 150 Local Employment Centres scattered around the province not only provide assistance and tools to facilitate job searches, they also direct people toward institutions and schools that offer education and training that meet their needs. The sectoral workforce committees are another institution that establishes skills standards or professional standards in each activity sector and helps define the demand for initial and continuing education and training. There are thirty of them in aerospace, forestry, rubber, culture, tourism, and other areas that ensure that certain types of adult learning and training are provided. Nevertheless, the integration of immigrants into the workforce remains a problem, especially for those who arrived in Canada already highly qualified yet can work in only entry-level jobs (Chicha and Charest, 2008). This situation creates frustration and the perception of discrimination; a clear policy for their full integration is needed.

The Role and Place of Adult Educators

Making education a top priority of Quebec as a society, improving achievement at all levels of education, and providing all students with qualifications for the labor market are among the objectives clearly stated by the Ministère de l'éducation du Québec (2000a). Despite awareness of the importance of adult education and the policies put forward by the government of Quebec, little has been said or done about the training and professionalization of adult educators themselves. They seem to be a neglected species that rarely, if ever, has the recognition their colleagues working in primary, secondary, public, and private schools enjoy. No specific diploma is required to work in the field, and as a profession, the occupation has no recognition. The Ministère de l'éducation du Québec seems to be aware that to lift obstacles to accessibility and ensure perseverance in continuing education, the quality of teaching for adults needs to be examined. Yet this awareness has not been translated into action. This position is odd, since the ministry recognizes that adults do not learn like children and need teaching methods tailored to

New Directions for Adult and Continuing Education • DOI: 10.1002/ace

their needs, objectives, and age. It is also surprising that the Ministère de l'éducation du Québec (2002a) put forward in its action plan some bold measures like the one that clearly states the need to "adapt a wider variety of types of training and places where training is provided."

Recently the government and policymakers seem to have acquired a new awareness of the importance of adult education for Quebec in order to maintain a competitive edge as a knowledge society (Conseil de la science et de la technologie, 2008). This awareness has translated into policies and strategic plans of action that, if followed, will certainly give impetus to adult education. The intention seems to be present, but whether it will translate to initiatives and actions that bring results is an open question.

Employment-related adult education and continuing education and training are shared responsibilities (government organizations, educational institutions, employers and the private sector, communities) that bring diversity to the field but also discrepancies.

Conclusion

The education system in Quebec, through government policies, funding, and the work of thousands of professionals and administrators, has achieved great results recently. It has brought a mainly French-speaking population that was far behind its Anglophone compatriots to a situation that is comparable in general. But it still faces many challenges, and vital tasks remain to be tackled. The dropout rate is still too high, which feeds illiteracy, unemployment, and lack of social integration. The integration of new immigrants from many different countries to the Quebec culture and society is another challenge. Finally, educating the workforce to ensure the ongoing renewal of skills is paramount in today's knowledge economy. The role and place of adult and continuing education is increasingly taken into account through strong policies like the Act to Foster the Development of Manpower Training. Nevertheless, many areas need dedicated and coordinated action among government, the private sector, and communities. Prior learning validation, recognition and encouragement of self-directed or informal learning, and greater participation, especially among the difficult to reach, are just a few of them. Adult education remains undervalued and underfinanced in Quebec. In its 2000–2003 strategic plan, little place was given to it, except for a mention that a "main complementary course of action [is the] revision of adult education programs" (Ministère de l'éducation du Québec, 2000a).

References

Béland, P. *Langue et immigration, langue de travail: éléments d'analyse, 2008.* Conseil supérieur de la langue française. Retrieved, September, 1, 2009, from http://www.cslf.gouv.qc.ca/publications/pubf228/f228.pdf.
Bélanger, P. *Adult Education: A Lifelong Journey: The Scope of the Government Policy on Adult Education and Continuing Education and Training. The Increasing Importance of*

Adult Education in Québec Education Policies. Queébec City: Ministère de l'éducation, Government of Quebec, 2002.

Bélanger, P., and Robitaille, M. *A Portrait of Work-Related Learning in Quebec.* Montreal: Université du Québec à Montréal, 2008.

Bouchard, G., and Taylor, C. *Fonder l'avenir: le temps de la conciliation. Rapport de la Commission sur les pratiques d'accomodement reliées aux différences culturelles.* Government of Quebec, 2008. Retrieved September, 1, 2009, from http://www.accommodements.qc.ca/documentation/rapports/rapport-final-integral-en.pdf.

Chicha, M.-T., and Charest, É. L' intégration des immigrants sur le marché du travail à Montréal; politiques et enjeux. *Choix,* 2008, *14*(2), 3–62.

Conseil de la science et des technologies. "Stratégie de recherche et de transfert de connaissances pour favoriser le développement de l'éducation et de la formation des adultes (Project)." Unpublished document. Quebec City: Government of Quebec, 2008.

Conseil supérieur de l'éducation. *L' éducation des adultes: partenaire du développement local et régional.* 2003. Retrieved September 1, 2009, from http://www.cse.gouv.qc.ca/FR/Download/index.html?id=dev reg&cat=dev-reg.

Conseil supérieur de la langue française. *The French Language in Québec: 400 Years of History and Life.* 2007. Retrieved September, 1, 2009, from http://www.cslf.gouv.qc.ca/F156ang asp.

Conseil supérieur de la langue française. *Le français langue de cohésion sociale.* Avis au ministre responsable de l'application de la charte de la langue française, 2008. Quebec City: Government of Quebec. Retrieved September 1, 2009, from http://www.cslf.gouv.qc.ca/publications/avis202/a202.pdf.

Inchauspé, P. *Vers une politique de formation continue: rapport final présenté à M. François Legault, ministre de l'éducation.* Quebec City: Government of Quebec, Ministère de l'éducation, 1999.

Institut de la statistique du Québec. *Immigration.* 2008. Retrieved September, 1, 2009, from http://www.stat.gouv.qc.ca/publications/referenc/quebec_stat/pop_imm/pop_imm_1.htm.

Livingstone, D. W. "Exploring the Iceberg of Adult Learning: Findings of the First Canadian Survey of Informal Learning Practices." *Canadian Journal for the Study of Adult Education,* 1999, *13*(2), 49–72.

Ministère de l'éducation du Québec. Gouvernement du Québec. *Strategic Plan of the Ministère de l'éducation for 2000–2003: Summary.* 2000. Retrieved September 1, 2009, from http://www.mels.gouv.qc.ca/ADMINIST/plan_strategique/PlanStrat0003/Anglais.pdf.

Ministère de l'éducation du Québec. *Government Policy on Adult Education and Continuing Education and Training: Learning Throughout Life.* 2002a. Retrieved September 1, 2009, from http://www.mels.gouv.qc.ca/REFORME/formation_con/Politique/politique_a.pdf.

Ministère de l'éducation du Québec. Gouvernement du Québec. *Action Plan for Adult Education and Continuing Education and Training 2002–2007: Learning Throughout Life.* 2002b. Retrieved on September, 1, 2009, from http://www.mels.gouv.qc.ca/REFORME/formation_con/Plan/plan_a.pdf.

Ministère de l'emploi et de la solidarité sociale. Gouvernement du Québec. *Stratégie d'intervention à l'intention des travailleuses et des travailleurs de 45 ans et plus.* Emploi Québec. 2003. Retrieved September 1, 2009, from http://www.emploiquebec.net/publications/pdf/00_imt_45ansplus.pdf.

Office québécois de la langue française. *Rapport sur l'évolution de la situation linguistique 2002–2007.* Montréal: Gouvernement du Québec, 2008.

Statistiques Canada. *Enquête sur la vitalité des minorités de langue officielle.* 2007. Retrieved September 1, 2009, from http://www.statcan.gc.ca/daily-quotidien/071211/dq071211a-fra.htm.

Stefanescu, A., and Georgeault, P. *Le français au Québec, les nouveaux défis.* Montréal: Les éditions Fides, 2005.

Tuijnman, A., and Boudard, E. (2001). *Enquête internationale sur la littératie des adultes. La participation à l'éducation des adultes en Amérique du Nord: Perspectives internationales.* Retrieved September 1, 2009, from http://www.statcan.gc.ca/pub/89-574-x/ 89-574-x1998001-fra.pdf.

MOHAMED HRIMECH *is professor of adult education at the Faculty of Education, Université de Montréal.*

5

The literature and pan-Canadian consultations involving adults with low literacy skills, immigrants and refugees, adults with HIV/AIDS, and those in remote Canadian communities all point to a health learning gap and a critical role for adult educators—a role that crosses all borders.

"More Universal for Some Than Others": Canada's Health Care System and the Role of Adult Education

B. Allan Quigley, Maureen Coady, Hélène Grégoire, Sue Folinsbee, Wendy Kraglund-Gauthier

Health and health care in Canada is a story of high ideals, complex policy agreements, moments of raging public controversy, and the creation of a national health system that is the envy of many other nations. Despite its many health care achievements, evidence is mounting that good health is far from being universally accessible to all Canadians. As we discuss in this chapter, following a three-year pan-Canadian study on health and learning, it became painfully clear to us that in far too many cases, one's ability and capacity to learn about health can have immediate—even life-and-death—consequences. We concluded that good health is not strictly a medical problem and not simply a governmental funding issue. Our conclusion was that good health is, above all, a matter of successful learning. Our study made it clear that adult education can play a key role in enabling people to maintain and improve their health. Yet we found that learning and health is a remarkably underresearched, underrecognized area within the ambit of adult education. Since the area of learning and health not only defies boundaries but is far larger and more complex than any policy, system, or program, we hope that these findings will encourage adult educators in Canada and beyond to become more involved in the critical issue of health and learning.

NEW DIRECTIONS FOR ADULT AND CONTINUING EDUCATION, no. 124, Winter 2009 © 2009 Wiley Periodicals, Inc.
Published online in Wiley InterScience (www.interscience.wiley.com) • DOI: 10.1002/ace.352

What We Studied and What We Found

Recent health research provides estimates that 30 percent of Canada's population—more than 9 million—are "unserved or underserved" (Pierre and Seibel, 2007, p. 3). Included in this estimate are marginalized populations that experience cultural isolation as well as geographical, social, and economic challenges. We first surveyed the health and learning literature relevant to Canada and then consulted with four groups of adults often considered part of these marginalized populations: adults with limited literacy skills, refugees and immigrants, adults living with HIV/AIDS, and those living in remote or rural areas of Canada.

While adult education has a history of working with each of these groups through a range of programs and advocacy actions, in both Canada and beyond, learning about one's health is rarely at the center of this work. Instead, health has largely been understood to be the domain of health professionals and health systems.

Canada has had a longstanding commitment to health and health promotion. In 1986, it was chief signatory to the Ottawa Charter for Health Promotion, an international landmark document on health promotion that advocated health equity. It asserted that health equity would be made possible by going beyond hospitals, emergency rooms, health care systems, and the medicalization of knowledge. Health promotion was being internationally recognized in the charter as a principal vehicle for "enabling people to learn [about their health], throughout life, [and] to prepare themselves for all of its stages" (World Health Organization, 1986, p. 3). It was "to be facilitated in school, home, work and community settings" (p. 3). It was internationally agreed in 1986 that "action is required through educational, professional, commercial and voluntary bodies, and within the institutions themselves" (p. 3).

Subsequent global charters on health promotion advocated the involvement of civil society as an essential aspect of health equity. In keeping with the spirit of those agreements, Canada has many examples of community-based health promotion initiatives, a few of which are discussed later in this chapter. Yet our pan-Canadian consultations on health and learning have reinforced that despite rhetoric on "enabling" and intentions to "increase options . . . for people to exercise more control over their own health" (World Health Organization, 1986, p. 3), little has changed for far too many. In practice, successes in addressing the social determinants of health are rare (Raphael, 2008).

Far from being "health enabled," one woman living in a rural area of Atlantic Canada told us: "Anyways you're supposed to trust what the doctor gives you. They are the doctors" (Folinsbee and others, 2007, p. 16). Despite advocating better health choices, the choice for another participant came down to "a choice to buy antibiotics or feed [her] kids" (Folinsbee, Kraglund-Gauthier, Grégoire, and Quigley, 2008b).

Many of the adults we consulted with live in poverty—one of the primary determinants of health. Ironically, while we were often told how inadequate "universal health care was," Canada's statistics note that Canada's poorest households "account for about 31% of the total expenditures on health care . . . almost double the utilization of the highest-income grouping" (Canadian Public Health Association, 2008, p. 7).

Nevertheless, Scriven and Speller (2007) cite examples where "grass roots activity has often sustained health promotion when government policy interest has waned" (p. 197). Here is the positive side of health resilience—a finding also borne out in our study. From our literature review and our consultations, we concluded that it is here—at the intersection where health learning occurs and community voice is raised—that adult education needs to play a far stronger role.

More partnerships for responsive policy formation need to be created between the fields of health and adult education. Health needs to be understood as more than the sum of a nation's systems, educational programs, and provision of services. Adult educators need to become stronger advocates, facilitators, researchers, and partners in addressing the range of determinants that contribute to the health of nations.

Canada's Health Care History

Following World War II, the international discourse on health became concentrated on issues of health care accessibility. Vast amounts were being spent in industrialized countries on health technologies and systems, yet many lacked access to even the most basic health services (Wass, 2000). In 1946, the World Health Organization introduced a new definition of *health* meant to address the limitations of a biological understanding of health. In this new definition, health was understood less as "the presence or absence of disease" but rather as "a resource for everyday life" (p. 2). This reframing ushered in a new era of Canadian health policy with a new focus on wellness and health promotion (Jackson and Riley, 2007).

In Canada, basic health care is considered a right, not a privilege. This began with a historic event many Canadians are proud to relate. In 1964, Tommy Douglas, premier of the prairie province of Saskatchewan, boldly introduced free hospital care for every Saskatchewan citizen. This highly controversial first step put Canada on the road to a publicly funded national health insurance system that made basic health services available to every permanent Canadian resident. However, Canada went well beyond the provision of improving access to health care systems. It championed a national health promotion model and tabled a document, *A New Perspective on the Health of Canadians*, known as the LaLonde Report (LaLonde, 1974), in parliament in 1974.

For the first time, the federal government had a health promotion policy to promote universal health. Health outcomes were seen as being influenced by a range of determinants, including lifestyle, environment, the organization of health care services, and human biology (World Health Organization, 2006). Amid mounting evidence that basic health needs could best be met through the greater involvement of people themselves, the 1978 Declaration of Alma-Ata introduced an international discourse on primary health care that advocated working with people through systems and programs to enable them to make informed decisions about their health.

Eight years later in Canada, "Achieving Health for All: A Framework for Health Promotion," also known as the Epp Report (Epp, 1986), expanded Canada's health emphasis from factors controlled by individuals to a focus on societal factors and conditions. The Epp Report recognized that lifestyle choices are not always a simple matter of individual choice; rather, choices often must be weighed within social and cultural structures. Rather than insisting that all Canadians make "good health choices," their options are often conditioned and constrained by factors such as poverty, unemployment, poor housing, and social and economic inequalities. Such social determinants for health have since expanded to include literacy, education, social justice, gender, and equity (World Health Organization, 2006). The Epp Report established that reducing inequities was fundamental to health promotion and universal health.

These concepts were enshrined in the Ottawa Charter for Health Promotion (World Health Organization, 2006), the first international agreement on health promotion. Again, Canada was a signatory and prime contributor. Enabling Canadians to increase control over their own health was to be promoted through five action streams: (1) building healthy public policy, (2) creating supportive environments, (3) strengthening community action, (4) developing personal skills, and (5) reorienting health services (Hawe and others, 1998; Raeburn and Rootman, 1998). Significantly for adult educators and learners alike, health inequalities were to be addressed through public participation and capacity building.

Throughout the 1980s, Canadian health promotion activity was stimulated or directly funded by the federal government at both the provincial and local levels. However, the 1990s saw an economic recession. Reduced federal spending, reduced federal leadership, and a decline in the influence of the federal government in health promotion were the results. Maintaining the same level of commitment to primary health care and health promotion strategies became a serious challenge. Largely motivated by public health threats, health promotion was restaged through efforts to strengthen the public health infrastructure (Jackson and Riley, 2007). Health promotion became a thrust for facilitating evidence-based decision making. Tools and mechanisms arose to assess the health impacts of federal programs. Compared with the earlier halcyon policy days, a narrowed, more medicalized health focus emerged (Millar, 2002), and health promotion saw the number of involved voices decline in health policies. Through to today, the voice of Canada's mainstream is now heard far more often than that of the marginalized in health discourse and policy formation.

New Directions for Adult and Continuing Education • DOI: 10.1002/ace

Voices from the Margins

In an effort to establish a research baseline for our work, our Adult Working Group began with an environmental scan and a state of the field review of health and learning in Canada (Folinsbee, Kraglund-Gauthier, Grégoire, and Quigley, 2006a, 2006b). We found considerable literature concerning health care and health-related issues, including a wealth of literature on the social determinants of health, but we found few connections between learning and health. The learning and developmental role that adult educators might play in promoting health was largely absent in the recent medical and health knowledge base. In 2006–2007, we sought to supplement the research knowledge base through the spoken experiences and recommendations of adults with low levels of literacy skills and adult immigrants and refugees in five provinces (Folinsbee, Kraglund-Gauthier, Grégoire, and Quigley, 2007). In our second year, 2007–2008, we held consultations with adults living with HIV/AIDS and those in rural and remote regions where fewer health services were provided and health risks were high. These were conducted in one Northern Territory and four provinces. Our objective throughout this three-year project was not to conduct generalizable research but to inform both practice and policy through consultations with these four marginalized groups.

Adults with literacy challenges and immigrants and refugees—along with their service providers—stated that health and learning was indeed a life-and-death issue. They described situations in which their own or another's health had been placed at risk because of a lack of literacy skills. They discussed the impact of literacy on workplace health and safety. They stressed their difficulties in improving their literacy skills when they were too busy working at low-wage jobs and acknowledged they were in low-waged jobs because their literacy skills were not sufficient for better employment. Far from making poor health choices, they repeatedly told us how poverty often made choices for them. They told us they often could not afford to buy healthy food for themselves or their families. Many sought medical attention, but without adequate drug subsidization, they were often unable to afford required medication.

Our consultations pointed to the difficulty that people with literacy challenges face in following doctors' directions and prescription instructions. Similar findings arose in our consultations. One adult with literacy challenges explained that "those papers [from the pharmacist] are too long," and "have too many big words" (Folinsbee, Kraglund-Gauthier, Grégoire, and Quigley, 2007, p. 16). The literacy challenged and immigrants and refugees alike stressed that they did not know what questions to ask the doctor, they felt doctors did not have enough time for them, and they felt intimidated by doctors. Literacy providers reinforced such perceptions and added that time spent with doctors was often insufficient for low-literate adults to make sure they truly understand diagnoses. On this point, we heard from participants that they often felt paralyzed and did not understand diagnoses, prescriptions, or the medical advice they were expected to act on. One participant described a miscommunication between her and her doctor in completing hospital forms that delayed her surgery, with permanent health consequences.

Across all of our consultations, participants and service providers spoke about the cultural insensitivity and discriminatory treatment that these groups often received. Race, socioeconomic status, sexual orientation, and HIV status were often cited. In one consultation, street-involved people—individuals who are "absolutely homeless and/or very precariously housed" and/or have access to shelter that is "poor quality, inadequate, or unstable" (Higgitt, Wingert, and Ristock, 2003, p. 14)—with literacy challenges told us that health care professionals often labeled them, and the public treated them as "nonhumans." The homeless and street involved were often either the last called or the not-called-at-all in hospital emergency rooms. In other examples, participants told us that people of color and Aboriginal people were not given thorough examinations and felt they were not respected (Folinsbee, Kraglund-Gauthier, Grégoire, and Quigley, 2007).

In 2007–2008, our second year of consultations, we saw the exasperation of those living with HIV/AIDS to access credible information about their illness. For some, an inability to learn was exacerbated time and again by literacy and language barriers (Folinsbee, Kraglund-Gauthier, Grégoire, and Quigley, 2008a). Others told us that health care professionals were often ignorant about HIV/AIDS, inevitably leading to negative, even tragic, health care experiences. Discrimination was named repeatedly. One consultation participant said the doctor listened to his heart with gloves on; another said the dentist examined his mouth while standing two feet away from him (Folinsbee, Kraglund-Gauthier, Grégoire, and Quigley, 2008a).

Across the consultations, participants raised issues of poverty, housing, food security, and inequitable access to health care and health knowledge. Our consultations in rural and remote areas revealed unique inequalities and pressures that inadequate services can bring on an entire community. The constant theme with all four populations was the importance of learning to happen. This learning was framed as a need for them to learn and as a need for community members, service providers, physicians, policymakers, and politicians to learn as well. For many participants, this learning needs to focus on "self-advocacy within the system, managing one's health, self-acceptance, and activism" (Folinsbee, Kraglund-Gauthier, Grégoire, and Quigley, 2008b, p. 25). Inaccessible health care, ineffective health promotion, and the lack of opportunity to learn their way toward better health were key issues.

Recommendations for Change

Participants in our pan-Canadian consultations made many recommendations. They repeated the need to reduce poverty, create affordable housing, and improve access to health-enhancing resources and health care services. Participants called for the recognition of credentials of foreign doctors so care capacity could be improved. They called for more health workshops and discussion groups, and sensitivity and awareness training for health providers. They recommended more language training and skills-upgrading opportunities, more trauma counseling for immigrants and refugees, and learning sessions for men about their health. But the recommendations and issues did not stop there. The practitioners and stakeholders who work with them told us how they often felt overwhelmed by the challenges they saw and how inadequately resourced they are.

It is well recognized that countries such as the United Kingdom, New Zealand, and many European nations have made health equity a high priority. In Sweden, perhaps the most cited example, "Social welfare policy is seen to be key to reducing health disparities" (Gardner, 2008, p. 36) While Canada has long focused on health equity, achieving it remains elusive. National health statistics indicate that differences in health outcomes of population groups are increasing and that "the social determinants of health . . . are responsible for almost half of the variation in health outcomes" (Canadian Public Health Association, 2008, p. 3). As a more global health phenomenon, the World Health Organization (2008) has stated that the "toxic combination of bad policies, economics, and politics is, in large measure, responsible for the fact that a majority of people in the world do not enjoy the good health that is biologically possible" (p. 1).

We ultimately concluded that the importance of health learning has not been sufficiently realized, but some Canadian health promotion initiatives in the past forty years could provide lessons on community learning and promise ways forward for the marginalized. For example, the Canadian Heart Health Initiative stimulated numerous health promotion activities at the provincial and local levels between 1986 and 1992. Today it is widely recognized as having "put new health promotion concepts into action" (Jackson and Riley, 2007, p. 216) by creating local, provincial, and national infrastructure that engaged collaboration between health, education, recreation, and environmental sectors, as well as chronic disease groups.

At a more regional level in Canada, a number of community self-care experiments show promise. For example, more than thirty-five youth health centers exist in schools in Nova Scotia, providing a wide range of health services and other supports for youth. Also in Nova Scotia, patient navigators in health care settings link people with the information and resources necessary to navigate the health system in order to maintain and improve their health (Ginn, 2008, p. 55). This concept is being expanded to include vulnerable populations such as seniors to help them navigate the complexities of systemic and community health services and supports. An example of truly engaging the marginalized, the Ontario Women's Health Network has adapted peer research approaches to create inclusive focus groups led by vulnerable and marginalized women in specific communities (Gardner, 2008).

Learning from the Margins

In our own consultations, participants praised certain community-based health centers they dealt with. In rural and remote areas where there were fewer health professionals or resources, the involvement of advanced nurse practitioners and, in rural Ontario, collaborative family health care teams were described as working well. Those singled out were invariably organizations that were sensitive to the needs of the marginalized. Interestingly, the constant theme among our four population groups was the importance of access to informal community systems of referral and local care. This is an important and hopeful outcome.

In one rural community in the Northwest Territories, we saw how only one Aboriginal woman could successfully coordinate health referrals and follow-up for all community members. In non-Aboriginal communities in Ontario and Nova Scotia, informal structures once again made all the difference. In sum, we saw that members of the four groups typically look to one another for support, but we also heard them insist they needed accurate, current information in plain language. We learned that mutual support among those in similar circumstances can contribute to a sense of self-efficacy, safety, and belonging. People affected by HIV/AIDS, for example, cited the importance of peers and support groups, crediting them as a "key component of [their] health and well-being" (Folinsbee, Kraglund-Gauthier, Grégoire, and Quigley, 2008a, p. 25). The resilience of mutual support was also seen in urban areas with, for instance, the homeless and people living on the street. It was seen again and again in smaller communities with few health resources and in rural and remote communities where personal isolation was having a serious impact on health and well-being.

Finally, health care providers themselves often experienced many of the stresses of isolation and lack of resources. We learned how the ways they shared effective practices and learned from one another enabled them to ensure the right people get the information they need in a way they understand. Herein lies hope.

Health, Learning, and the Twenty-First Century

If the promise of universal health care is to be realized in Canada and beyond our borders, the wisdom and strength of seasoned, informal leaders and the resilience of the marginalized need to be recognized, supported, and further researched. The ability of informal community leaders, communities, and coalitions and the learned capacities of those dealing with low literacy, language barriers, geographical isolation, and HIV/AIDS are places we need to look to in order to improve health around the globe. The expertise and abilities of the marginalized should not be on the margins but at the center of the research and policy agenda for the twenty-first century.

We became aware of an important link between health and adult education. Our consultations reinforced that strengthening the link between health and adult education, and particularly the linkages between health and formal and informal learning, can provide a way forward in helping people maintain and improve their health.

The challenge for adult educators is to bring the voices of those who experience the greatest challenges to health into the discussion. If this were done, "improving health, addressing inequities in health, building and sustaining healthy communities and health partnerships, and helping people gain control over the conditions that affect their health" (Folinsbee, Kraglund-Gauthier, Grégoire, and Quigley, 2006b, p. 46) could be far better addressed. Working collaboratively with the health sector, adult education can play a key role in enabling citizens to learn their way toward better health.

References

Canadian Public Health Association. "Canadian Public Health Association response to the World Health Organization (WHO) Commission's Report: Closing the Gap in a Generation. Health Equity Through Action on the Social Determinants of Health." 2008. Retrieved September 10, 2008, from http://www.cpha.ca/uploads/briefs/cpha_who_sdoh_e.pdf.

Epp, J. "Achieving Health for All: A Framework for Health Promotion." 1986. Retrieved June 23, 2007, from http://www.frcentre.net/library/AchievingHealthForAll.pdf.

Folinsbee, S., Kraglund-Gauthier, W. L., Grégoire, H., and Quigley, A. *Health and Learning Environmental Scan.* Vancouver, BC: Health Learning Knowledge Centre and Canadian Council on Learning, 2006a.

Folinsbee, S., Kraglund-Gauthier, W. L., Grégoire, H., and Quigley, A. *State of the Field Review: Health and Learning.* Vancouver, BC: Health Learning Knowledge Centre and Canadian Council on Learning, 2006b.

Folinsbee, S., Kraglund-Gauthier, W. L., Grégoire, H., and Quigley, A. "Adult Work Group Cross-National Consultations on Health and Learning: Report." Antigonish, NS: National Collaborating Centre for the Determinants of Health, 2007.

Folinsbee, S., Kraglund-Gauthier, W. L., Grégoire, H., and Quigley, A. "Adult Work Group's Cross-National Consultations on Health and Learning: Final Report on Adults Affected by HIV/AIDS." Vancouver, BC: Health Learning Knowledge Centre and Canadian Council on Learning, 2008a.

Folinsbee, S., Kraglund-Gauthier, W. L., Grégoire, H., and Quigley, A. "Summary of the Adult Work Group's Inverness Consultations on Health and Learning with Adults Living in Rural and Remote Areas." Vancouver, BC: Health Learning Knowledge Centre and Canadian Council on Learning, 2008b.

Gardner, B. "Thinking Globally, Acting Locally About Health Reform." *Making Waves,* 2008, *18*(3), 35–39. Retrieved September 10, 2008, from http://www.cedworks.com/files/pdf/free/MW180335.pdf.

Ginn, J. "Community Connections." *Making Waves,* 2008, *18*(3), 53–57. Retrieved September 10, 2008, from http://www.cedworks.com/files/pdf/free/MW180353.pdf.

Hawe, P., and others. "Multiplying Health Gains: The Critical Role of Capacity-Building Within Health Promotion Programs." *Health Promotion International,* 1998, *39*, 285–295.

Higgitt, N., Wingert, S., and Ristock, J. "Voices from the Margins: Experiences of Street-Involved Youth in Winnipeg." 2003. Retrieved November 18, 2008, from http://ius.uwinnipeg.ca/pdf/Street-kidsReportfinalSeptember903.pdf.

Jackson, S., and Riley, B. *Health Promotion in Canada, 1986–2006.* Toronto: Centre for Health Promotion/University of Toronto Press, 2007.

LaLonde, M. *A New Perspective on the Health of Canadians.* Ottawa: Health and Welfare Canada, 1974.

Low, J., and Theriault, L. "Health Promotion Policy in Canada: Lessons Forgotten, Lessons Still to Learn." *Health Promotion International,* 2008, 23(2), 200–206.

Millar, J. "Playing on the Same Team? Health Promotion and Population Health in Canada." *Health Promotion Journal of Australia,* 2002, 13(2). Retrieved November 14, 2004, from http://www.healthpromotion.org.au/journal/previous/2002_2/05.html.

Pierre, N., and Seibel, H. "Frontline Health: Beyond Barriers. Report of the Ottawa Roundtable. 2007 (p. 3). Retrieved August 27, 2008, from http://www.cprn.org/documents/49117_EN.pdf.

Raeburn, J., and Rootman, I. *People Centred Health Promotion.* Hoboken, N.J.: Wiley, 1998.

Raphael, D. "Getting Serious About the Social Determinants of Health: New Directions for Public Health Workers." *IUHPE Promotion and Education,* 2008, 15(3), 15–20.

Rekart, M. L., and others. "HIV Prevalence and Risk Among Street-Involved Persons." International Conference on AIDS, 1990, 6(225).Vancouver: International Aids Society.

Scriven, A., and Speller, V. "Global Issues and Challenges Beyond Ottawa: The Way Forward." IUHPE *Promotion and Education,* 2007, 14(4), 194–198.

Wass, A. *Promoting Health: The Primary Health Care Approach.* (2nd ed.) Orlando, Fla.: Harcourt, 2000.

World Health Organization. "Preamble to the Constitution of the World Health Organization as Adopted by the International Health Conference, New York, 19–22 June, 1946." In *Official Records of the World Health Organization.* Geneva: World Health Organization, 1946.

World Health Organization. "Ottawa Charter for Health Promotion: 1986, 2006." Retrieved September 10, 2008, from http://www.euro.who.int/AboutWHO/Policy/20010827_2.

World Health Organization. *Closing the Gap in a Generation: Health Equity Through Action on the Social Determinants of Health.* Geneva: World Health Organization, 2008.

B. ALLAN QUIGLEY *is professor in the Adult Education Department, Saint Francis Xavier University, Antigonish, Nova Scotia, and cochair of the Adult Working Group for the Health and Learning Knowledge Centre, Canadian Council on Learning.*

MAUREEN COADY *is assistant professor in the Adult Education Department, Saint Francis Xavier University, Antigonish, Nova Scotia.*

HÉLÈNE GRÉGOIRE *is adjunct assistant professor at the Dalla Lana School of Public Health, University of Toronto, and cochair of the Adult Working Group for the Health and Learning Knowledge Centre, Canadian Council on Learning.*

New Directions for Adult and Continuing Education • DOI: 10.1002/ace

SUE FOLINSBEE *is a consultant and researcher-coordinator of the Adult Working Group for the Health and Learning Knowledge Centre, Canadian Council on Learning.*

WENDY KRAGLUND-GAUTHIER *is instructional designer and editor for the Continuing and Distance Education Department at Saint Francis Xavier University, Antigonish, Nova Scotia, and a researcher-writer for the Adult Working Group for the Health and Learning Knowledge Centre, Canadian Council on Learning.*

New Directions for Adult and Continuing Education • DOI: 10.1002/ace

This chapter summarizes the area of critically oriented environmental adult education, focusing on the relationship between historical contextual factors and Canada's current leadership in environmental adult education. A comparison of Canadian and American student environmental activism demonstrates how contextual factors shape nonformal learning and activism.

Critical Environmental Adult Education in Canada: Student Environmental Activism

Elizabeth Lange, Aaron Chubb

It is no accident that a large number of humorists have emanated from Canada. Taking the slow path of a negotiated divorce from the British Empire, an ongoing contentious negotiation with Aboriginal and French incumbents, and never seeing itself as an economic, political, or military world power, Canada has developed a self-deprecating sense of humor and irreverence. Paradoxically, Canada is also known for politeness and understatement, perhaps given this history of negotiation and continual adaptation to newcomers, yielding one of the most multicultural populations in the world. In these and other ways, Canada's reality has been shaped by a political economic context that is different from the United States. In a far-flung country with small clusters of inhabitants in isolated regions amid challenging geography, a sense of collectivity was required for simple survival and national cohesion. Furthermore, Canada maintained connective tendrils with Europe and former Commonwealth countries, which have in part shaped its parliamentary processes, predisposition toward social democracy, and critical intellectual tradition. While not overlooking Canada's racist, classist, and gendered policies and practices, some political and cultural characteristics have also come from the incorporation of Aboriginal forms of governance and social relations, only now being affirmed (Saul, 2008). Corresponding to these contextual factors, the historical roots of the Canadian adult education field have also been organic to specific regions, collectivist, and community based, most often located in social movements.

NEW DIRECTIONS FOR ADULT AND CONTINUING EDUCATION, no. 124, Winter 2009 © 2009 Wiley Periodicals, Inc.
Published online in Wiley InterScience (www.interscience.wiley.com) • DOI: 10.1002/ace.353

Today recent polls have indicated that the Canadian public considers the environment and climate change as their top concern (De Souza, 2007), perhaps eclipsed only by recent economic fears. In keeping with the historical responsiveness of adult educators, environmental adult education (EAE) is widespread across North America. However, this area of adult education has been underreported and undertheorized. In this chapter, we argue that the most rapid and recent theorizing of EAE in North America has been occurring in Canada. The contextual factors that help to explain this are Canada's collectivist ideology, strong regionalism, accommodation of diversity, criticality, persistence of international connections, and the availability of state funds for the voluntary, nongovernment sector. We explore environmental student activism on both Canadian and American campuses, concluding that differences in funding and structure relate to contextual differences, with distinct outcomes for social justice and environmental education and action. Finally, we argue that the global environmental challenges present numerous new entry points for the practice of adult and higher education. Infusing environmental and sustainability learning into existing formal and nonformal adult education programs, as well as recognizing the importance of activism, particularly student activism, as a legitimate and vital form of adult education, are two responses to this challenge.

Canada's Historical Context

Canada's unique historical context and the ways in which these political, economic, ideological, geographical, cultural, and social realities have intersected have shaped Canadian dreams, dispositions, and conduct. A brief description of some key factors will provide important background for discussing the development of EAE in Canada.

One overwhelming reality for Canada early in its history was the need to bind the small, historically isolated communities of newcomers together across a vast and daunting geography. The building of a national railway, the policy of dispossessing indigenous people of their traditional territories, and the constant encouragement of immigration were three initiatives for ensuring settlement and control over the land, largely for protecting it from the covetous American gaze (Careless, 1970). The federal government had responsibility for immigration, national protection, and economic development, but its ability to meet regional needs was stretched. This unleashed the need for local social capital—trust, mutual aid, shared knowledge, and political skills (Epp and Whitson, 2001)—which manifested as the trend toward regional protectionism. Early in the twentieth century, small, local communities developed traditions of self-directed, participatory governance and cooperative enterprise to overcome natural geographical barriers, build economic well-being, and in many cases resist exploitative financial interests of large companies: in mining, timber, agriculture, fishing, and the railways. This was one origin of Canada's regionalism and ideological pre-disposition toward social democracy.

Subsequently the four pillars of the Canadian social safety net that developed after the 1930s were unemployment insurance, medicare, social assistance, and the Canada pension plan. Pressure from social movements on the government was integral to the development of the Canadian social welfare state, eventually expanded to include family allowance payments, minimum wages and other labor legislation, student loans, crop insurance, workers' compensation, and state-owned utilities, to name a few programs. Similarly, different levels of government regularly made funds available to voluntary nonprofit groups, that is, the civil sector, as a way to meet regional needs, foster civic participation, and undercut more radical demands—even if these groups were in turn critical of government. In a backhanded way, this provided legitimate routes for criticism and dissent, but it also tempered it as organizations strove to keep their government funding. Nevertheless, social movements, and the adult learning programs embedded in them, have been a distinctive element in the development of Canada's political and social life. Many adult educators agree that social movements have been a key entry point for adult educators that ought to be maintained (Welton, 1993; Collins, 1991; Hall, 2006), and we argue that this ought to include environmental social movements.

A second key reality has been Canada's reliance on the extraction and exportation of rich natural resources, resulting in a staples economy (Innis, 1995). Canada did industrialize and then diversify its manufacturing sec-tor, but more recently, it has moved through the Fordist stage of deskilling and mechanizing primary resource jobs and then the neoliberal phase of moving many manufacturing jobs offshore. Attracting foreign investors into commodity production and offering favorable tax regimes, long-term access to raw resources, and relaxed environmental standards has meant that small commodity producers and workers have been squeezed out of their gener-ational homes to become service sector workers. This has resulted in a pro-found deterioration of community self-reliance, cooperative initiatives, and environmental protection (Epp and Whitson, 2001). This has become another critical entry point for adult sustainability educators.

Antecedents and Canadian Approaches to Environmental Adult Education

It is intriguing that the theory and practice of environmental education for adults has been so underdeveloped in North America, despite the visibility of the environmental movement since the 1960s, extensive media coverage of environmental issues, and fervent U.N. support for environmental edu-cation. Despite three waves of calls for environmental education in the adult education field each decade since 1970, as well as the vigorous development of K-12 environmental education for forty years, environmental concerns did not penetrate the adult education field until the 1990s (see Lange, forthcoming a).

The beginning of the environmental movement in North America is commonly marked from Rachel Carson's publication of *Silent Spring* in 1962, scientifically documenting the impact of DDT on songbirds. By 1970, the first international Earth Day was celebrated in New York, the U.S. Environmental Protection Agency was formed, the U.S. Clean Air Act was passed, and Greenpeace was born in Vancouver, Canada, to protest nuclear testing in Amchitka off Alaskan shores. The first National Environmental Education Act was passed in 1970, and the North American Association for Environmental Education (NAAEE) was formed in 1971, largely focusing on K–12 teachers and adult educators in nonformal venues, such as naturalist clubs, state parks, museums, and zoos. Evidence is widespread that nonformal environmental education for adults is continuing to take place in widely dispersed sites and sectors. Yet this is not reflected well in adult education literature and research. Various explanations suggest that the politicized climate surrounding environmental issues, the discomfort of working with activists, the dominant individualist and psychological focus of adult education, and the lack of knowledge regarding environmental and scientific discourse all discourage engagement (Taylor, 2006; St. Clair, 2003).

Despite the early development of American environmental initiatives, a recent examination of the literature indicates that Canadians are now leading the development of EAE theory and practice. One primary factor for this has been the tight link between Canadian adult educators, international adult education organizations, and European environmentalism. For instance, after the publication of the Brundtland Report (United Nations World Commission on Environment and Development, 1987) on sustainable development, the International Council for Adult Education (ICAE), a global partnership of adult educators who promote adult learning as a tool for informed participation in civil society, adopted sustainable development as part of its mandate. Three Canadians—Budd Hall, Darlene Clover, and Paul Belanger—have been pivotal members of ICAE since its inception in 1973, serving in leadership capacities and overseeing the headquarters in Toronto, Canada.

In 1991, ICAE established the Learning for the Environment Programme (LEAP), the "only global network that provided a place of encounter for adult educators who were working within an ecological framework" (Clover, 2004, p. vv). As part of LEAP, Darlene Clover and Brazilian Moema Viezzer organized an EAE gathering as part of the 1992 Rio Earth Summit that produced Agenda 21, a comprehensive blueprint for a global partnership. Out of this LEAP-sponsored gathering, the first treaty on EAE, Environmental Education for Sustainable Societies and Global Responsibility, was adopted. In 1997, at the fifth UNESCO international conference on adult education, environmental issues were on the agenda for the first time (Clover, 2006). The resulting report, the *Hamburg Declaration and Agenda for the Future,* and the handbook, *Environmental Adult Education: From Awareness to Action,* mark an international watershed providing clear principles and a working definition to guide EAE. Thus, the early promotion and conceptualization of EAE came through these international agencies. Canadian participation at the international level gave impetus to much needed theorizing and the uptake of EAE practice in North America.

In the 1990s, a critical mass of literature began to appear. *Convergence,* the journal of ICAE, published in Toronto, produced special environmental issues in 1989, 1992, 1995, and 2000. This was the first significant conduit of environmental education messages into the North American adult education field, as was the North American Association for Popular Education, which Clover coordinated for five years. Two seminal theorists, whose publications represent the turning point in academic-based literature, are Canadians Edmund O'Sullivan and Darlene Clover. Edmund O'Sullivan (1999) merges deep ecology with critical ecopsychology, ecospirituality, and ecofeminism to build a comprehensive vision for adult education. Practices for facilitating the formation of an ecological consciousness were elaborated in an edited collection by both O'Sullivan and Marilyn Taylor (2004). Critical ecofeminist Darlene Clover (1995, 1998) developed some of the earliest theoretical and pedagogical foundations for critical EAE, in keeping with Canada's critical intellectual tradition. These theorists also helped establish the Transformative Learning Centre of the Ontario Institute for Studies in Education, University of Toronto, as a base for research on transformative learning through environmental action. To give just a sample of the diversity in research now occurring, other Canadians writing on EAE include Belanger (2003), who integrates environmental discourse with lifelong learning; Sumner (2005), who examines the global pressures on rural communities that compromise their sustainability and self-reliance; and Duguid, Mündel, and Schugurensky (2007), who examine the learning aspects of volunteerism related to sustainability as part of citizenship education. Lange (2004; in press a, in press b) fuses radical ecology with sustainability education into the development of a restorative as well as transformative pedagogy. Tan (2004) advocates for an inclusive antiracist environmental discourse, drawing on the wisdom of newcomer immigrant groups.

All of these contributions are consonant with the critical and social movement tradition in Canadian adult education. Most of the theorist-practitioners highlight important links between environmental and social justice issues in relation to neoliberal globalization. Furthermore, their critical analysis centers on the economic and ideological roots of the current environmental crisis rather than on individual behavior change, attitudes, or scientific knowledge that is part of the dominant environmental education approach. Clover (2003) is especially adamant that the field "make[s] concrete links between the environment and social, economic, political, and cultural aspects of people's lives" (p. 10) and that they use critical and transformative pedagogies. Many of these educators also advocate for EAE to be community based, starting from the learners' lived experiences and catalyzing links to local, national, or global activism (Clover, Follen, and Hall, 1998; Clover and Follen, 2004). Similarly, many of these environmental adult educators are working to reinvigorate participatory local governance, cooperative initiatives, and cultural diversity, and they resist further incursions of global capital that compromise community sustainability. To underscore the importance that state and other collectivized funding has had for Canadian voluntary organizations, the following case study on student environmental activism highlights the contextual differences shaping Canadian and American adult education.

Student Environmental Activism for Campus Sustainability: Nonformal Adult Education

The literature on environmental and sustainability projects in the formal education sector, particularly university campuses, is relatively large. As well, many universities have come a long way over the past twenty years, for example in recycling, particularly when these changes meet administrative needs for fiscal savings or for a green public image (Mansfield, 1998). However, the more complex issues of sustainability in relation to educational goals for fostering a sustainable society have yet to be addressed (Gruenewald, 2003; Sipos, Battisti, and Grimm, 2008). The U.N. Decade of Education for Sustainable Development, 2005–2014, has called attention to "the bridges that must be built between academia and community needs" (Sipos, Battisti, and Grimm, 2008, p. 72). In this regard, student environmental activists are often connected to wider communities, which make them ideal change agents in providing bridges required for the transition to a truly sustainable university and society. Yet there is considerably less literature on student-led campus activism, specifically their relationships to broader environmental and sustainability social movements and how their work for change brings about positive effects in adult and higher education. We agree with Cunningham (1992) that activists, in this case student activists, are some of the least studied and most underappreciated nonformal adult educators in North America. This is curious since student activists are ideally located within both environmental movements and formal educational institutions, thereby bridging education and action. Indeed, there is now a movement within a movement—the sustainable campuses movement within the environmental movement—where student activists are taking the lead in pressuring and educating for change (Mansfield, 1998; Shriberg, 2003).

One example of the change needed is the Western university's hierarchical, and now neoliberal, structure that often breeds top-down and behaviorist approaches to sustainability. This runs counter to the dialogical model of adult education and the goals of equal power relationships within social movements. Furthermore, when sustainability initiatives cost money, administrators often do not respond, despite professed principles, until pressure is created by student social movements. Breaking exclusivity contracts with major corporations like Coca-Cola is one example. While many students see a company complicit in the murder of union activists in Colombia or in the pollution and depletion of fresh water in India, university administration, and even a student union administration, see the loss of a lucrative source of income. Tufts University provides an example of encouraging energy conservation by students through a social marketing approach that involves behavioral incentives (Marcell, Agyeman, and Rappaport, 2004). This approach is more manipulation than education toward sustainability goals, however. In contrast, students at Tufts and hundreds of other universities have organized to remove Coca-Cola from their campuses, simultaneously participating in the wider social movement (Klein, 2001; Rogers, 2008). Thus, it is where the interests of administration and the interests of students collide—over questions of sustainability and strategy—that the sites most in need of social movement pressure and adult learning for a sustainable campus are revealed. Interestingly, Beringer (2006) claims that it has been bottom-up student pressure that has induced 80 percent of the colleges in the United States to adopt recycling programs.

Student activism is not limited to resistance; efforts are often made to create exemplars for learning what a sustainable campus and society can look like, from informal learning related to renovating student housing for energy sustainability, campus collective gardens, bicycle co-ops, and Food Not Bombs groups to extensive nonformal education opportunities through conferences, speakers, and workshops. While these practices can be found on both American and Canadian campuses, the dynamics of student movements in both countries are significantly different in terms of structure, funding, regional context, and community connections, providing an interesting comparison of learning and activism.

A Comparative Study: Funding, Structure, and PIRG Student Movements

One of the primary differences between American and Canadian campus environmentalists revolves around sources of funding. Given Canada's history of relatively large amounts of funding to the arts and voluntary nonprofit sectors, including adult education, these resources are often directly or indirectly available for social movement activity. Large funding cuts to the voluntary sector did occur in the 1990s, but Canadian social and environmental programs still receive more funding relative to American programs, given the drastic cuts under Presidents Reagan and George W. Bush. American environmental student activists generally need to rely on small amounts of state funding, which can quickly disappear as the political climate changes (Zimmerman and Halfacre-Hitchcock, 2006), becomes unstable and centrally controlled by an umbrella nongovernmental organization (Dawson, 2007), or is influenced by grants from large foundations such as the Rockefeller Foundation and the Pew Charitable Trusts, whose funding criteria implement its own agendas (Lewis, 2003; Oja Jay, 2007).

Public Interest Research Groups (PIRGs), started in the United States by Ralph Nader in the 1970s, have successfully lobbied for laws to protect the consumer and environment alike. The U.S. model is for a state-level PIRG to accumulate funds from student levies and other fundraising efforts for redirection back to various campaigns. While the PIRGs have been instrumental in influencing state and federal policy, student-led action for sustainability on individual campuses is not a priority. On campuses with PIRG chapters, paid staff often lead the actions and thus are criticized for dampening student initiative (Strauss, 1996). By 1981, although U.S. PIRGs had been in existence for over a decade and existed in one out of every nine campuses, only fifty universities across the United States had recycling programs prior to 1996. It was not until student movements began addressing this issue that mass mobilization for sustainable campuses began. For instance, the CEAC Catalyst Conference in 1992 drew over seventy-six hundred students, and by 1995, over two thousand student environmental organizations existed on campuses, with over twenty-seven hundred campuses instituting recycling programs after 1996. Over the past several decades, as student activists have begun to focus more on single-issue campaigns, broad umbrella groups such as the American PIRGs have begun to fade in prominence from one in nine campus-based PIRGs to one in twelve by 2000 (Levine and Cureton, 1998) and in the decade since there has been no reversal to this trend.

Canadian PIRGs were organized shortly after their American counterparts, starting in Ontario. Yet the student environmental movement in Canada lacks a large student population and is more regionally dispersed, resulting in the slower development of a critical mass for sustainability. While the number of American PIRGs is now declining, Canadian students are busy forming new ones with PIRGs in 30 percent of Canadian universities. Having a strong collective identity at the local level has allowed some independence for Canadian student environmentalists. This independence is also related to sources of funding.

Although Canadian PIRGs were inspired by their American counterparts, they have undertaken a radically different model of organizational structure and funding. Students in Canada often maintain much more control over their PIRG, with student-run boards of directors and hired staff. Since a relatively steady source of funding exists, largely from student levies and government funding, and given that it is controlled by students, it is often made available for social action. Thus, the student body and student organizers easily recognize the benefits of supporting a campus PIRG.

Many successful student projects through Canadian PIRGs are local ones that produce tangible changes. Almost every Canadian PIRG supports one or more sustainability projects. There are now over forty-six student or student-community environmental groups funded by PIRGs where "students can confront [an] issue without having to take on the entrenched institutional system" (Hirsch, 1993, p. 35, cited in Zimmerman and Halfacre-Hitchcock, 2006), including campus gardens and student-run composting programs. Canadian PIRGs also support efforts that directly confront institutional power, including anti–Coca Cola campaigns and ecojustice solidarity groups related to indigenous self-determination. The key differences between the Canadian PIRG grassroots approach and the American PIRG lobbying approach are hands-on community leadership, the provision of critical adult education, and broader social movement connections. While Canadian PIRGs provide more opportunities for critical education among students as well as activist formation, they often lack the long-term institutional direction required for campaigns that have a direct impact on provincial or federal policy. Most recently, movements have formed around environmental problems with global implications, such as the Alberta tar sands, which has attracted funding from larger American foundations. There is evidence that this may lead to similar compromises that some American environmentalists have faced with unstable project funding (Oja Jay, 2007).

Conclusion

Historically, Canadian adult education has been rooted in social movements, cooperative enterprises, regional needs, and participatory politics. Canada has sought to provide collective funding for regionally distinct needs and self-reliance. In addition, its international links have shaped the existence of a broad ideological spectrum as well as influenced the development of adult education, including EAE. Student environmental activism, particularly on campuses, has been similarly shaped by these factors of regionalism, collective funding, and participatory, community-based models of organization.

However, given its historic reliance on raw resources, commodity production, and manufacturing, all reliant on an oil and gas carbon economy, Canada now faces the challenge of unplugging from an environmentally debilitative economic system to rise as a global leader in energy alternatives and other socio-economic elements that will generate a sustainable society. This is a critical fork in the road for Canada as a nation and for adult educators. The challenge has created numerous new entry points for the practice of adult education. Significant entry points include infusing environmental and sustainability learning into nonformal adult education programs, from antiracism education and rural development programs to literacy and professional development programs. Another significant entry point is supporting local groups that are countering the forces of neoliberal globalization that undercut community sustainability and are attempting to create viable alternatives. In formal education sites, recognizing the importance of activism,

particularly student activism, as a legitimate and vital form of adult education effective for encouraging positive change and building bridges to the
larger community is much needed. Adult education has a legacy of fostering
transformative, inclusive, and critically oriented adult learning in environmental and social justice movements, as well as in countless community-
based organizations, which should be enhanced by making the learning
component visible. Finally, capturing and theorizing these activities within
the literature of adult education can generate knowledge and courage, as well
as profile role models and pedagogies of mobilization for a sustainable future.

References

Belanger, P. "Learning Environments and Environmental Education." In L. H. Hill and
    D. Clover (eds.), Environmental Adult Education: Ecological Learning, Theory and Prac-
    tice for Socioenvironmental Change. New Directions for Adult and Continuing Educa-
    tion, no. 99. San Francisco: Jossey-Bass, 2003.
Beringer, A. "Campus Sustainability Audit Research in Atlantic Canada: Pioneering the
    Campus Sustainability Assessment Framework." International Journal of Sustainabil-
    ity in Higher Education, 2006, 7(4), 437–455.
Careless, J.M.S. Canada: A Story of Challenge. Toronto: Macmillan of Canada, 1970.
Carson, R. Silent Spring. Boston: Houghton Mifflin, 1962.
Clover, D. "Theoretical Foundations and Practice of Critical Environmental Adult Edu-
    cation in Canada." Convergence, 1995, 28(4), 44–54.
Clover, D., Follen, S., & Hall, B. The nature of transformation: Environmental, adult and
    popular education. Toronto, ON: University of Toronto, 1998.
Clover, D. "Environmental Adult Education: Critique and Creativity in a Globalizing
    World." In L. H. Hill and D. Clover (eds.), Environmental Adult Education: Ecological
    Learning, Theory and Practice for Socioenvironmental Change. New Directions for Adult
    and Continuing Education, no. 99. San Francisco: Jossey-Bass, 2003.
Clover, D. (ed.). Global Perspectives in Environmental Adult Education. New York: Peter
    Lang, 2004.
Clover, D. "Policy Development, Theory and Practice in Environmental Adult Educa-
    tion." Convergence, 2006, 39(4), 51–54.
Clover, D., and Follen, S. "The Nature of Transformation: Developing a Learning
    Resources for Environmental Adult Education." In D. Clover (ed.), Global Perspec-
    tives in Environmental Adult Education. New York: Peter Lang, 2004.
Clover, D., Follen, S., and Hall, B. The Nature of Transformation: Environmental, Adult
    and Popular Education. Toronto: University of Toronto, 1998.
Collins, M. Adult Education as Vocation. New York: Routledge, 1991.
Cunningham, P. "From Freire to Feminism: The North American Experience with Crit-
    ical Pedagogy." Adult Education Quarterly, 1992, 42(3), 180–191.
Dawson, A. "Greening the Campus: Contemporary Student Environmental Activism."
    Radical Teacher, 2007, 78(19), 19–23.
De Souza, M. "Environment Biggest Public Concern, Poll Finds." 2007. Retrieved August 6,
    2008, from http://www.canada.com/edmontonjournal/news/ story.html?id=802cac42-
    dfe5–4c5a-965f-d5ddd3f37067.
Duguid, F., Mündel, K., and Schugerensky, D. "Learning to Build Sustainable Commu-
    nities Through Volunteer Work in Urban and Rural Settings: Insights from Four
    Case Studies." Paper presented at the Joint International Conference of the Adult Edu-
    cation Research Conference and the Canadian Association for the Study of Adult
    Education, Halifax, NS, June 2007.

Epp, R., and Whitson, D. *Writing Off the Rural West*. Edmonton, AB: Parkland Institute and University of Alberta Press, 2001.

Gruenewald, D. "The Best of Both Worlds: A Critical Pedagogy of Place." *Educational Researcher*, 2003, 32(4), 3–12.

Hall, B. "Social Movement Learning: Theorizing a Canadian Tradition." In T. Fenwick, T. Nesbit, and B. Spencer (eds.), *Contexts of Adult Education*. Toronto: Thompson Educational Publishing, 2006.

Hirsch, D. "Politics Through Action." *Change*, 1993, 25(4), 19.

Innis, H. *Staples, Markets, and Cultural Change: Selected Essays*. Montreal: McGill-Queen's University Press, 1995.

Klein, N. *No Logo*. London, U.K.: Flamingo, 2001.

Lange, E. "Transformative and Restorative Learning: A Vital Dialectic for Sustainable Societies." *Adult Education Quarterly*, 2004, 54(2), 121–139.

Lange, E. "Fostering a Learning Sanctuary for Transformation in Adult Sustainability Education." In J. J. Mezirow and E. Taylor (eds.), *The Handbook of Transformative Learning in Practice*. San Francisco: Jossey-Bass, forthcoming a.

Lange, E. "Environmentally-Oriented Adult Education." In C. Kasworm, A. Rose, and J. Ross-Gordon (eds.), *The Handbook of Adult and Continuing Education*. Thousand Oaks, Calif.: Sage, forthcoming b.

Levine, A., and Cureton, J. "Student Politics: The New Localism." *Review of Higher Education*, 1998, 21(2), 137–150.

Lewis, T. L. "Environmental Aid: Driven by Recipient Need or Donor Interests?" *Social Science Quarterly*, 2003, 84(1), 144–161.

Mansfield, W.H.I. "Taking the University to Task." *World Watch*, 1998, 11(3), 24–30.

Marcell, K., Agyeman, A., and Rappaport, J. "Cooling the Campus: Experiences from a Pilot study to Reduce Electricity Use at Tufts University, USA, Using Social Marketing Methods." *International Journal of Sustainability in Higher Education*, 2004, 5(2), 169.

Oja Jay, D. "Can Pew's Charity Be Trusted? US Foundations Give Millions to Canadian Environmental Groups." *Dominion: Canada's Grassroots Newspaper*, November 25, 2007, 48.

O'Sullivan, E. *Transformative Learning: Educational Vision for the 21st Century*. London: Zed Books, 1999.

O'Sullivan, E., and Taylor, M. (eds.). *Learning Toward an Ecological Consciousness*. New York: Palgrave Macmillan, 2004.

Rogers, R. "The Campaign to Stop Killer-Coke." 2008. Retrieved October 15, 2008, from http://www.killercoke.com.

St. Clair, R. "Words for the World: Creating Critical Environmental Literacy for Adults." In L. H. Hill and D. Clover (eds.), *Environmental Adult Education: Ecological Learning, Theory and Practice for Socioenvironmental Change*. New Directions for Adult and Continuing Education, no. 99. San Francisco: Jossey-Bass, 2003.

Saul, J. R. *A Fair Country: Telling Truths About Canada*. Toronto: Viking Canada, 2008.

Shriberg, M. "Is the 'Maize-and-Blue' Turning Green? Sustainability at the University of Michigan." *International Journal of Sustainability in Higher Education*, 2003, 4(3), 263–276.

Sipos, Y., Battisti, B., and Grimm, K. "Achieving Transformative Sustainability Learning: Engaging Head, Hands and Heart." *International Journal of Sustainability in Higher Education*, 2008, 9(1), 68.

Strauss, B. H. "The Class of 2000 Report: Environmental Education, Practices, and Activism on Campus." New York: Nathan Cummings Foundation, Environment Program, 1996.

Sumner, J. *Sustainability and the Civil Commons*. Toronto: University of Toronto Press, 2005.

Tan, S. "Anti-Racist Environmental Adult Education in a Trans-Global Community: Case Studies from Toronto." In D. Clover (ed.), *Global Perspectives in Environmental Adult Education*. New York: Peter Lang, 2004.

Taylor, E. "The Greening of the Adult Education Academy." In S. Merriam, B. Courtenay, and R. Cervero (eds.), *Global Issues and Adult Education*. San Francisco: Jossey-Bass, 2006.

UNESCO. (1997). Adult education: The Hamburg declaration and the agenda for the future. *Proceedings from CONFINTEA V: The Fifth International Conference on Adult Education*. Hamburg, Germany: UNESCO.

UNESCO. (1999). Adult environmental education: Awareness and environmental action. In the series *Adult Learning and the Challenges of the 21st Century*, Booklet 6a from the *Fifth International Conference on Adult Education (CONFINTEA V)*. Hamburg, Germany: UNESCO.

United Nations World Commission on Environment and Development. *Our Common Future* [Brundtland Report]. New York: Oxford University Press, 1987.

Welton, M. "Social Revolutionary Learning: The New Social Movements as Learning Sites." *Adult Education Quarterly*, 1993, 43(3), 152–164.

Zimmerman, K. S., and Halfacre-Hitchcock, A. "Barriers to Student Mobilization and Service at Institutions of Higher Education: A Greenbuilding Initiative Case Study on a Historic, Urban Campus in Charleston, South Carolina, USA." *International Journal of Sustainability in Higher Education*, 2006, 7(1), 6–15.

ELIZABETH LANGE *is assistant professor of adult and higher education in the Department of Educational Policy Studies, University of Alberta, Edmonton.*

AARON CHUBB *is a master's student in adult and higher education in the Department of Educational Policy Studies, University of Alberta, Edmonton.*

7

Within the context of the community college system in Canada, this chapter presents a case study for faculty development within which this development is treated as an adult education initiative.

Learning to Teach: An Illustrative Case from the Canadian Community College System

Ellen Carusetta, Patricia Cranton

In both the United States and Canada, higher education faculty have access to voluntary faculty development activities through continuing professional education departments, but rarely are preparatory programs available for those preparing to become faculty. Faculty development initiatives are only infrequently grounded in adult education principles and practices, though some writers advocate this. As well, there is little overlap between the primary faculty development association, Professional and Organizational Development, and the various adult education associations, such as the Canadian Association for the Study of Adult Education and the American Association for Adult Continuing Education; neither is there very much crossover in the literature between teaching and learning in higher education and adult education. Yet faculty who are learning about teaching are, or could be, engaged in adult education. This chapter provides one instance of how community college faculty in a Canadian college system are treated as adult learners and how they bring their knowledge of adult education theories and skills into their practice.

Despite the lack of connection in the literature or between organizations, in Canada, particularly at the community college level, we do have some good models of how faculty can be enrolled in adult education–focused programs that prepare them to teach. This type of approach could be incorporated

New Directions for Adult and Continuing Education, no. 124, Winter 2009 © 2009 Wiley Periodicals, Inc.
Published online in Wiley InterScience (www.interscience.wiley.com) • DOI: 10.1002/ace.354

into other adult education programs, many of which already have college faculty enrolled. We first provide an overview of the community college system in Canada for readers unfamiliar with it. We then focus in on the community college system in the province of New Brunswick, where both of us have been involved in preparing college faculty for teaching for many years. We describe the nature of this instructor development program (IDP), which is integrated into the adult education program offerings at the University of New Brunswick. We then present an illustrative case from, first, the perspective of an educator in the program (Patricia Cranton) and, second, from an administrator in the same program (Ellen Carusetta). Finally, we discuss the broader implications of treating faculty development as an adult education initiative—that is, as a program that espouses the theory and practice of adult education.

Overview of Community College Systems in Canada

Community colleges in Canada differ from those in the United States. Canadian colleges evolved from technical and vocational schools that existed in each of the provinces. These colleges are diploma- rather than degree-granting institutions and are mandated to prepare employees in applied fields of study. The formation of the community college system was based not only on the provision of training programs, but also on some general principles that were widely believed to be of benefit to Canadian society. These principles included a focus on accessibility through open admissions policies, provision of preparatory programs, promotion of diversity, flexibility of scheduling, and an emphasis on teaching rather than research. The colleges were designed to be responsive to government direction and changes in the economy and to provide specialized services as needed in their local communities (Rogers, 2004).

To understand the structure of the community college system in New Brunswick, one needs some understanding of how the responsibilities for higher education in Canada are delineated. In Canada, the provinces and territories have sole responsibility for education, and although the federal government plays a major role in higher education, there is no federal government department of education or higher education. Each province or territory assigns responsibility for higher education to a member of the elected government cabinet or delegates specific parts of the higher education spectrum to different government departments (Jones, 1997). Governance of the community college systems cannot be generalized across provinces. Some provinces have a strong tradition of community-based decision making, and others operate under the direct authority of the provincial government (Dennison, 1995). Also, most provinces or territories have intermediary bodies that provide the government with advice concerning the coordination and regulation of higher education.

New Directions for Adult and Continuing Education • DOI: 10.1002/ace

The Community College in New Brunswick

The New Brunswick Community College (NBCC) was established in 1974 as a corporation with a board of governors and five citizen advisory boards. In 1980, the government took over direct control of NBCC, placing it under the supervision of a government department, the Department of Continuing Education (Brown, 1997; New Brunswick Community College, 2005). The college fell under the auspices of different iterations of government departments and as of 2006 was located with the Department of Post-Secondary Education and Labour. NBCC is a network of the College of Craft and Design and eleven separate campuses—six Anglophone and five Francophone.

In the NBCC system, priority is given to hiring faculty with considerable experience working in the field in which they teach (for example, carpentry, plumbing), so many faculty members, especially in the trades, have no first university degree. The community college prepares people for work in the trades, technologies, hospitality industry, and some areas of health care. A condition of employment for instructors is that they participate in the IDP. Part-time instructors and those wanting to find full-time employment in the college may also take the program.

The IDP began in the mid-1970s, using adult and higher education consultants from Quebec and Ontario to plan and teach in the program. The resulting program had a one-week residential component, consisting of courses in adult learning, communication, and adult education methods. It was staffed by faculty who had expertise in adult education theory and practice.

In 1989, the Department of Adult and Vocational Education in the Faculty of Education at the University of New Brunswick (UNB) entered into a formal arrangement with the Department of Advanced Education and Training to provide in-service education to Anglophone community college instructors. Under this contract, IDP participants could transfer courses taken in the program into a certificate or bachelor of adult education program. Some participants also go on to take graduate degrees in education or adult education.

No major changes occurred in the IDP until 2006, when the government Department of Post Secondary Education and Training determined that it could better serve instructors by offering some of the IDP courses themselves. An agreement was reached whereby the NBCC itself offers three courses, and UNB offers the other three courses. A transfer agreement allows all courses to be accepted into either the certificate or bachelor in adult education program at the university.

The IDP consists of two intensive three-week summer sessions, a practicum that takes place between the two summer sessions, and three other courses from the undergraduate adult education program. Many courses are available online as well as face-to-face, but teaching methods courses have

New Directions for Adult and Continuing Education • DOI: 10.1002/ace

been held in face-to-face summer sessions until recently. During the first summer and also as part of their practicum, participants learn the skills and techniques of teaching. They practice making presentations in a microteaching format, create course outlines and objectives, and develop tests for their students—the nuts and bolts of teaching. When they arrive for the second summer, most are relatively comfortable with the basics of classroom and shop or field teaching, though there are always more topics they want to explore in these areas. All courses in the program follow an adult education model; they are learner centered and discussion based. Learners are encouraged to be self-directed and responsible for their learning; they participate in the selection of topics in some courses and engage in self-evaluation in others. Collaborative and constructivist learning are encouraged; learning projects, writing assignments, and in-class presentations offer flexibility and choice. Participants come to see themselves as adult educators as well as adult learners. Recognizing that their own students include both young adults and more mature learners, these mature students become comfortable with adapting teaching and learning strategies to suit their classes at the college level.

Community college faculty work within a system that includes mandated curriculum (to meet the needs of industry) and policies and procedures that predetermine assessment strategies, attendance, contact hours, preparation time, and the like. These issues are discussed extensively in the IDP, and participants find interesting and innovative strategies for maintaining their stance as adult educators in a context that has many constraints against doing so. Many of participants' previously held habits of mind and social expectations about the role of educators are called into question during the program. They learn to challenge and critically question the system within which they practice.

An Illustrative Case: An Educator's Perspective

We begin at 8:00 A.M. on the first day after the Canada Day holiday (July 1). People are looking around uncertainly, searching for familiar faces and for the right classroom. Many have driven two hours to get here, meaning they left home at 6:00 A.M., and most are clutching coffee cups. There are more men than women milling around, and they range in age from the late twenties to the early sixties. Most, men and women alike, wear knee-length shorts and a T-shirt, though there are some jeans and, now and then, a summer dress or skirt. Almost everyone was together the previous summer, though there may be one or two people who missed a year and are new to the group. As people find others whom they know, there are handshakes, claps on the back, and occasionally even a hug. The noise level in the room begins to increase with the joking, laughter, and stories.

As the professor, I take advantage of New Brunswickers' love of storytelling and begin the morning by asking everyone to tell a story of an amazing teaching experience from their previous year. The stories inevitably focus on students who overcame great odds to succeed or those who were ready to drop out but made it in the end. I ask, "What did you do to help?" or "What do you think made a difference?" and they talk about making connections with their students and developing good relationships. Caring comes through strongly, though they may not use that word, instead speaking with a kind of toughness sometimes associated with the camaraderie of the trades.

We then talk about the different kinds of learning they promote in their classrooms and shops, and I attach the labels *instrumental, communicative,* and *emancipatory* to their descriptions. I ask them to draw a picture that shows how the three kinds of learning are related and interrelated. Usually at least one tree is drawn, with instrumental knowledge being the roots, communicative knowledge being the trunk, and emancipatory learning being the leaves. But there are also sailboats, houses, cars racing down a road, birdhouses complete with birds—every summer, there are depictions I had not seen previously.

At some point on this first day (which goes from 8:00 A.M. until 1:00 P.M.), we plan the topics together for the first half of summer school. Participants work in groups of three or four individuals each and list all of the topics they are interested in exploring. They then pare down this list and come to consensus on their top four or five topics. The discussion is animated, and, as always with this group, there is a lot of laughter and joking. We bring the small group topics together in the larger group and, after much discussion, create a list of the topics for the first six or seven classes. In this way, together we create our course. The planning process is repeated again for the second half of the course, by which time everyone knows what they would still like to spend time on.

After this, we settle into a routine. There are usually readings related to the topics of the day, and we discuss those readings, bringing in illustrations from everyone's experiences. I design learning activities—group work, pairs work, individual exploration, and reflection—related to the topic, readings, and discussion. These activities include role play, critical debates, simulations, skits, and other experiential activities (one day, we changed a tire in the parking lot; another day, we dismantled and reconstructed the cupboards in the classroom). We go outside for class on fine days, and we sometimes go to the art gallery, an exhibit, or a downtown improvisational theater, finding ways to connect these activities to our understanding of teaching and learning. People are fully immersed in the stuff of adult education. They read it, think about it, do it, and talk about how it applies to their teaching.

Participants engage in a learning project outside class time, either independently or with others. The nature of this project is completely open, and I encourage arts-based projects, journals, autobiographies, interviews of stellar teachers—anything that brings another level of meaning to their

New Directions for Adult and Continuing Education • DOI: 10.1002/ace

practice. Grading is based on self-evaluation. I ask people to select a grade that represents their learning from all aspects of the course—class activities, readings, discussions, and their learning project—and simply give me that grade with a brief explanation of their choice. There is no negotiation, and no power relations are involved. I submit the grade they give me. I do make comprehensive comments on their learning projects, but this is unrelated to their grade unless they choose to take my comments into account in determining their grade.

A tension always exists between the nature of their teaching (primarily in the trades and technologies, instrumental knowledge) and my teaching about teaching (communicative knowledge). We explore this fully, examine it from many different angles, and take it apart and put it back together again. A few years ago, the group created what they called the ICE model (instrumental, communicative, and emancipatory knowledge) and presented this in a bar graph. In some contexts, the I part of the bar would dominate, and in others the C part of the model would be stronger, but always, in all contexts, all three (I, C, and E) were present.

Every summer, several sessions are related to challenges people face within the system: policies and procedures, administrative requirements, resources, and the like. We critically question and challenge the system boundaries, and most often we construct strategies that people intend to use when they return to the college in the fall. Three weeks is not a long time in the larger scheme of things, but it is an intensive time since we meet daily for five hours and engage in a great deal of introspection and exploration of who we are as teachers and what it means to be an adult educator.

An Illustrative Case: An Administrator's Perspective

I understood from the beginning that the government's main reason for bringing the instructor development program to the university was to provide a teaching credential for their faculty in the most practical and efficient way they could. My goals for the faculty members were to introduce them to philosophies of adult learning and engage them in adult teaching practices. I hoped to take them away from the "banking" form of education (Freire, 1970) they were used to and lead them to question the traditional teacher-centered practices in the college system. I both taught in the program and administered it for the faculty of education. The college faculty are, to this day, my favorite students. I consider myself an advocate for them. In trying to achieve my goals, I often encountered resistance on the part of community college administration. I illustrate two particular cases.

My first challenge came when I tried to revamp the practicum the participants completed between the first and second summers. The previous practice had been for faculty members to have their department head or another administrator act as their practicum mentor. These mentors were rarely cognizant of adult education practices. They would watch the participants teach, videotape a class, and discuss their teaching practices with them. I realized the power relations inherent in this arrangement and worked to change the process to one in which graduates of the program became mentors for new instructors. In doing this, I took some of the control over teaching practices away from college administrators. After a lengthy discussion on the benefits of a true formative evaluation and a reminder that the university was contractually given control of the academic regulations associated with the program, I succeeded in changing the practicum. After the changes, many instructors expressed their relief. They were intimidated by the presence of administrators in their classes. They felt their jobs were in jeopardy, and the educative experience of openly discussing teaching was lost.

A second major challenge occurred when the government joined the distance delivery bandwagon. As is often the case, they went full tilt and thought every course we offered should be delivered by distance. I understood their reasons. They wanted their faculty to experience distance delivery so they would embrace the new technologies and teach with them. They also knew there would be a cost saving for them. People could take courses on their own campuses, cutting down on the travel costs associated with the program. I am an advocate of using distance technologies, but I also believe the first consideration should be good pedagogy. After teaching in and watching the participants interact in the summer sessions, I knew a great deal would be lost if all the courses were changed to distance format and the summer experience was abandoned. In their intense summer experiences, they learned a great deal through their interactions with others from different campuses. They developed friendships and professional networks that lasted long after summer school ended. This was very evident when they returned for the second summer. And, of the utmost consideration for me, teaching methods and strategies could be truly effective only in a face-to-face environment. Again, I put my case to the college administration. This time I had agreement with at least some of the administration. They had seen the positive changes in their faculty and had come to value the summer school experience. We were able to compromise, and the methods courses remained in the two summers in a shortened time frame. All of the elective courses were offered in a rotation by distance delivery.

Implications

Adult education is a field that not only advocates specific learner-centered practices, but is also, and perhaps more important, a field that advocates social change and ideology critique. As can be seen in the other chapters in this volume (for example, Chapters One, Three, Six, and Eight), social change has long been at the center of Canadian adult education. Mezirow (2000) emphasizes the importance of adult learning emphasizing "contextual understanding, critical reflection on assumptions, and validating meaning by assessing reasons" (p. 3). Brookfield (2005) takes this further when delineating the centrality of critical theory to adult learning. He suggests that a theory of adult learning originating in the general concerns of critical theory helps us to investigate dominant ideologies, illuminate how the spirit of capitalism distorts everyday relationships, and, most important, understand how people identify and oppose the ideological forces and social processes that oppress them. A critical theory of adult learning, he writes, "is inevitably also a theory of social and political learning" (p. 31). Grounding learning about teaching in higher education within the foundations of adult education has several implications.

Viewing college faculty as adult learners and engaging them in self-directed, learner-centered, collaborative, and social and institutional change endeavors is a good first step in working toward much-needed reform in higher education (where traditionally educators transmit information to students and test them on retention). If we want institutions of higher education to engage people in critical thinking, creative leadership, and innovation—so important in our current global social structures—then faculty need a deep understanding of their roles as educators in moving in this direction.

Power relations come into play within the systems themselves. Often colleges and universities engage in professional development through in-service workshops and courses offered by their faculty for their faculty. To truly engage people, it is important to remove them, either physically or conceptually, or both, from where they feel constrained by the policies and philosophies of their parent institution. Faculty need to be able to explore new ways of thinking without fear of recrimination.

On a much larger scale, power relations in the world today—among races, cultures, countries, and political regimes—have led to war, unrest, poverty, torture, oppression, and fear. Educators and institutions of higher education are responsible for addressing these issues. For this to happen, we need educators who are aware of power structures, critical of prevailing governments and social norms, and willing and able to encourage their learners to do the same. Situating learning how to teach in the field of adult education where such discussions are the norm can move us in that direction.

Another current and pressing global issue is how to address and reverse the damage we have done to the environment (see Chapter Six, this volume) on a scale that is greater than changing the kind of lightbulbs we use or the number of plastic shopping bags we use. The future is dependent on being able to see from different perspectives and develop entirely new paradigms for how we live in the world. Yet colleges are more likely to maintain the status quo through the dissemination of existing knowledge than the creation of new knowledge. Again, faculty whose thinking is grounded in adult education, with its emphasis on social change, critical theory, and post-structuralism, are going to be better able to lead education into addressing these essential issues.

References

Brookfield, S. D. *The Power of Critical Theory*. San Francisco: Jossey-Bass, 2005.

Brown, S. A. "New Brunswick." In G. A. Jones (ed.), *Higher Education in Canada: Different Systems, Different Perspectives*. New York: Garland, 1997.

Dennison, J. D. *Challenge and Opportunity: Canada's Community Colleges at the Crossroads*. Vancouver: UBC Press, 1995.

Freire, P. *Pedagogy of the Oppressed*. New York: Continuum, 1970.

Jones, G. A. "Introduction." In G. A. Jones (ed.), *Higher Education in Canada: Different Systems, Different Perspectives*. New York: Garland, 1997.

Mezirow, J. "Learning to Think Like an Adult." In J. Mezirow and Associates (eds.), *Learning as Transformation: Critical Perspectives on a Theory in Progress*. San Francisco: Jossey-Bass, 2000.

New Brunswick Community College. "Modernizing the New Brunswick Community College." 2005. Retrieved February 7, 2008, from www. Gnb.ca/0105/NBCCDiscussionPaperEnglish.pdf.

Rogers, N. *Exemplary Practices in Community Development Research Report*. Ottawa: Association of Canadian Community Colleges, 2004. (ED 491 099)

ELLEN CARUSETTA is professor of adult education at the University of New Brunswick.

PATRICIA CRANTON is professor of adult education at Penn State University Harrisburg.

8

This chapter discusses four distinctive features of community development in Canada: focus on learning, use of media and the arts, international initiatives, and feminist leanings.

From Manifesto Days to Millennium Days: Canadian Perspectives on Community Development

Leona M. English

It is just about impossible to find an adult education department in Canada that does not have a critical social justice orientation, quite often oriented to community development. Many of the faculty identify themselves with the local and or global activist community, and they see their work as merging learning and justice concerns to build up the community sphere. This is not surprising since the roots of adult education in Canada are socialist oriented and specifically grounded in community development concerns. One has only to think of the social gospel influences in developing Farm Radio and Frontier College and of Roman Catholic social teaching's role in initiating the Antigonish movement to realize that Canadian adult education is distinct in both its roots and emphases. Consequently, Canadian practitioners and academics are concerned with understanding and grappling with issues in communities such as the First Nations, African Nova Scotians, and immigrant and urban factory workers.

In this chapter, I first provide an overview of community development in Canada and a description of its roots. From there, I turn to four distinctive facets of Canadian community development: the focus on adult learning, the role of media and the arts, the international perspective, and use of a feminist lens.

New Directions for Adult and Continuing Education, no. 124, Winter 2009 © 2009 Wiley Periodicals, Inc.
Published online in Wiley InterScience (www.interscience.wiley.com) • DOI: 10.1002/ace.355

Overview of Community Development in Canada

The operative understanding of community development in Canada is very much influenced by the work of the United Nations and, in turn, influences it. The United Nations sees community development as

> the process by which the efforts of the people themselves are united with those of governmental authorities to improve the economic, social, and cultural conditions of communities and to enable them to contribute fully to national progress. This complex process is made up of two essential elements: the participation by the people themselves in efforts to improve their level of living, with as much reliance as possible on their own initiative; and the provision of technical and other services in ways that encourage initiative, self-help and cooperation [United Nations, 1963, n.p.].

In this sense, Canadians often use *community development* to refer to domestic and international efforts to build capacity in communities, which can be loosely defined as existing between the individual and the public sphere. Key to our understanding is the dual role of grassroots people and of institutions, including government, to support the people and their initiatives. There is no doubt that provincial and federal governments play a role in this country and work alongside people to help them move forward.

The Canadian context is often seen to be communal, democratic, and quasi-socialist, as evidenced by the quality of our social programs and our education system. Government is a large presence in Canada, assuming primary responsibility for the care of its people, to the point of dedicating a community development division within a major federal department, Human Resources and Social Development Canada, and of also establishing a national rural secretariat. Our Canadian cultural and political context has been heavily influenced by a traditionally socialist government that has funded community-based and grassroots activity, though arguably at a decreasing level. Although there are erosions in our social fabric, community still seems to be an emphasis and collective concern. This trend is no accident; it is discernable and historically traceable.

Roots of Community Development in Canada

Adult education and community development have long been entwined in the Canadian academic and practitioner mind-set. We have a movement for adult education that was developed in large measure by a collective mind-set, which evolved out of a nexus of religious and educational development impulses. Like the Highlander Folk School and the civil rights movement in the United States, the well-known Antigonish movement in eastern Canada, for instance, was a blend of progressivism, religious fervor, and education, mixing learning with organizing for cooperatives and collective action.

New Directions for Adult and Continuing Education • DOI: 10.1002/ace

Set in the heart of a small Roman Catholic institution, St. Francis Xavier University, the Antigonish movement pushed education and progress through study clubs, lectures, People's Schools, and print materials. The movement is often seen as a highlight in North American community development because of its radicalism for the time and its unique blend of community education and activism. (See also Chapter Three.)

Michael Welton, a Canadian historian of adult education, has published extensively and critically on the Antigonish movement. His writings, specifically *Knowledge for the People* (1987), *The Life and Times of Father Jimmy* (Lotz and Welton, 1997), and his biography on the life of Antigonish movement leader Father Moses Coady, *Little Mosie from the Margaree* (2001), have chronicled the educational dimensions of some of our best-known Canadian social and development movements, all of which have strong learning aspects.

In western Canada, early adult education leaders like Ned Corbett also heralded the cause of community development. As president of the burgeoning Canadian Association for Adult Education (CAAE), Corbett, a Presbyterian minister who was heavily imbued with the fervor of the social gospel, put forward the Manifesto of the Canadian Association for Adult Education in 1943. This document highlighted social responsibility, collective action, and radical work for change. As leader of the association, Corbett was striving to find a postwar direction for the organization in the wake of the Great Depression. The manifesto was a document that, according to Friesen (1994), "pushed Canada's adult education movement sharply to the left" (p. 171). As a response to overwhelming geography, diverse economic needs, and educational dreams, this manifesto was intended to set a justice direction for the CAAE for the next several decades (Selman, Cooke, Selman, and Dampier, 1998). Led by what Friesen calls "populists, community organizers, social gospel idealists, democrats" (p. 174), this organization heralded a leftist orientation that continues today.

The manifesto (Corbett, 1943) was not Corbett's only contribution. He also started the National Farm Radio Forum to bring farm and rural education to people in a disparate and far-flung land. Farm Radio was an intense educational program that enjoined radio broadcasts with study clubs and print materials; a marker of its success is that it was adapted internationally (Selman, Cooke, Selman, and Dampier, 1998, p. 49). Simultaneously, in western Canada, prairie populism and the social gospel contributed to other Canadian community development initiatives such as the National Film Board (NFB) and Citizens' Forum, all of which have concentrated on increasing knowledge and learning.

These historical influences have meant that our country and its community development activity are heavily influenced by an adult learning focus (English, 2005a). Clear in each of these historical cases is that Canadian adult education has grown from the roots up with a very socialist streak that has made our adult education sphere political in orientation. We have

New Directions for Adult and Continuing Education • DOI: 10.1002/ace

had a creative fusion of politics, economics, and culture that continues to this day.

Adult Learning Focus

Historically and to the present, a strong element of most community development initiatives here is an intense adult learning component. Within the Antigonish movement, for instance, the workers who were part of its Women and Work Program were the beneficiaries of a number of adult education efforts. The program was directed for ten years by a Sister of Martha, Sister Marie Michael Mackinnon, and aided by another Sister of Martha, Sister Irene Doyle (Neal, 1998). Be it with the print materials that they used for study clubs and the involvement of capable and motivated educators, or with the use of libraries, these sisters were actively engaging in a nonformal learning campaign. And their intentionality was clear. Sister Marie Michael, fully aware of her own abilities and responsibilities, saw herself as working with Tompkins and Coady, not for them. She used the study club for teaching everything from beekeeping to home improvements, all part of her plan to give women control of their lives and an income with which to run them. Sister Marie Michael's career was characterized by a number of initiatives including hosting a local radio program during which she read and discussed books on air.

There has consistently been a culture of strong learning and teaching in our movements (Selman, Cooke, Selman, and Dampier, 1998). The term *social movement learning* (as distinct from "*learning in social movements*"), for instance, has come to be identified with Canadian Budd Hall (Hall and Clover, 2005), who popularized the term in North America. Spurred by decades of promoting community development and learning, Hall has been a Canadian leader in combining learning, activism, and research in the community. Currently director of a community development institute at the University of Victoria in British Columbia, it was he who coined the term "*participatory research*" (Hall, 1975) in the early 1970s as a result of his collaborative work in Tanzania. Along the way, he founded the International Participatory Research Network, which operated throughout the world during the 1970s, 1980s, and 1990s as a way of promoting participatory action research as a bonafide educational methodology for advancing community development research.

The strong focus on learning continues through research into learning and power in local women's organizations, which reveals that a significant portion of time in women's grassroots community development organizations is spent on informal and nonformal education related to economic issues, funding, governance, and lobbying (English, 2004). Adult educators have concentrated on learning for women on welfare who are returning to work (Andruske, 2001) and in the environmental movement (O'Sullivan, 1999), especially with regard to Clayoquot Sound in British Columbia where the rainforests and ocean are compromised environmentally (Walter, 2007).

New Directions for Adult and Continuing Education • DOI: 10.1002/ace

Social movement learning has even been the focus of the newly formed Canadian Council on Learning, a federal body designed to promote learning across Canada.

Learning continues to predominate in research and interest in Canada, as evidenced in a special issue of the *Canadian Journal for the Study of Adult Education* (2007), which profiles the findings of a number of research studies directed by David Livingstone and his colleagues at Ontario Institute for Studies in Education through a federally funded research project (2003–2007), The Changing Nature of Work and Lifelong Learning in the New Economy (known as WALL), which succeeded an equally intensive (1997–2002) study on New Approaches to Lifelong Learning (NALL). Much of the learning that NALL and WALL have pursued and documented has been informal and nonformal, and a considerable amount has occurred in the nonprofit and community sector. One of the articles in the CJSAE collection, for instance, is a case study using interview data that show how volunteer learning is integral to community sustainability for four community-based organizations addressing issues such as farming, healthy living, wind power generation, and housing cooperatives (Duguid, Mündel, and Shugurensky, 2007). This study contributes to the understanding of social movement learning and especially to the vital role this learning plays in strengthening our collective capacity to be sustainable.

Our Canadian perspective shows how learning can be deliberately and consciously integrated into community development. These initiatives have been furthered by our national government's commitment to funding for research in adult education and development and through publicly funded universities and financial and social support for adult learning through libraries, the national broadcaster, and a vibrant news media sector.

Media and the Arts

Along with promoting community development learning through research, media and the arts have historically played a strong role in our country's community development, with the exemplar being the creation of the National Film Board in 1949 by the federal government. The NFB's first director, John Grierson, helped establish film councils and use documentary film to educate and organize (see Selman, Cooke, Selman, and Dampier, 1998). One NFB project, the Challenge for Change series, was begun in Fogo, Newfoundland, in 1966. This project was conducted in concert with the local university and had community developers put filmmaking in the hands of the rural people, who were instructed to use it as a tool for self-assessment, education, and organizing. This use of film for change was replicated around the world. Along with sponsoring the NFB in filmmaking and libraries, the government continues to fund the Canadian Broadcasting Company as the nation's broadcaster, with a mandate to profile all regions of the country.

New Directions for Adult and Continuing Education • DOI: 10.1002/ace

The use of film and theater to assist in community education has continued in many regions. Carole Roy (2004), for instance, has studied the use of community theater among older women activists, the Raging Grannies, to promote peace. More recently, she has been studying film festivals as a radical means to educate the public (Roy, 2008). Roy is interested in the increasing public phenomenon of collective viewing of documentary films through organized festivals as a new form of social movement learning, which is transforming communities across Canada. (Chapter Two, this volume, showcases examples of using media to educate and make changes in northern Canada.)

Meanwhile, educators such as Butterwick and Selman (2003) have been using community and participatory theater as a way to promote adult education for those directly involved in community action. They used an extensive drama workshop process to bring community activists together to relate their experiences of coalition within feminist community groups. The interpersonal tensions that the drama reveals are not the story, however; for Butterwick and Selman, the actual theater process is the important piece in that it surfaces development issues in alternative ways and has the potential to sustain activists for the long haul. Similarly, Clover and Markle (2003) have been examining the adult education role of the visual and performing arts in effecting justice in the community. Arts-based initiatives, as they have shown, are key to understanding informal learning processes in the community.

These examples demonstrate how media and the arts can be used to unite and build a national identity and create change. Canada continues to have widespread public and government support for many of these media-related initiatives, and we continue to have adult education researchers and practitioners who are interested in integrating media in various forms into community development projects.

International Focus

A third emphasis of community development in Canada has been its global reach. One only has to think of the involvement of Canadians in UNESCO; examples include John Kerans's and Paul Belanger's leadership within that organization. Roby Kidd's founding of the International Council of Adult Education is also quite notable, along with Budd Hall's and Paul Belanger's terms as secretary general of this globally influential association. Not surprisingly, the council was housed in Canada for many years. Similarly, through our Canadian International Development Association, we have been promoting learning and international development for a long time.

In terms of women and learning on an international scale, Canadian adult educators have made a significant contribution. Angela Miles's study (2002) of women in social movements and globalization has made the links between women and development clearer. Patti Gouthro (2004) and others have looked at women's learning in Jamaica, Maureen Ryan has studied women's community development and learning in Grenada (Ryan and English, 2004), and English (2005b) has studied women who are involved in international adult education. Canadian women have been active in the Association of Women in Development and at UNESCO conferences such as Confintea. They have been there and made a worthwhile contribution in these organizations and have had a strong voice in Convergence and in other internationally focused journals.

One cannot forget that the Women's Institutes were begun in Canada in 1897 (see Chapter Three for a detailed description of the Women's Institutes). The institutes, a worldwide phenomenon, provide a place for women to gather, learn, and socialize. The Canadian founder, Adelaide Hoodless, was influenced by her own family experiences and convictions to expand the movement across the world (Chapman, 1952). In addition to learning household skills and knowledge, the women learned community participation, organizing, and political processes.

There is no doubt that international engagement has been a hallmark of Canadian community development. This is echoed in the continued Canadian presence in U.N. educational initiatives and our strong engagement in adult education internationally.

Feminist Focus. Also of note in Canada is the number of scholars who brought a strong and analytical feminist perspective to bear on their community development interests. They can be characterized as focusing less on learning in higher education, classrooms, and conventional settings and more on learning in community development and for global social change. Feminist theorists such as Angela Miles (1995), for instance, have worked to strengthen women's solidarity around the globe, with their own emphases on integrated feminisms that work together rather than in separate spheres.

Of special note in a Canadian context is the growing body of related research on immigrant women and learning. An emergent field of work examines the social contexts for immigrant women in Canada. Brigham and Walsh (2005), Mirchandani (2004), Mojab (2000), and Maitra and Shan (2005), for instance, look at the interlocking systems of oppression for women in this sector: race, class, and gender play into the social location of immigrant women. In an interesting study of learning from unpaid housework among Chinese immigrants, Liu (2007) brings to light the gendered and classed dimensions of this learning and how it has a special impact with immigrants.

Other adult educators have looked at women's groups such as Aboriginal women (Graveline, 2005), Thai women (Walter, 2004), and second-language learners (Ciccarelli, 1999). Slade, Luo, and Shugurensky (2005) add that these women use numerous informal learning strategies to improve their employment opportunities. Of special note here is the use of strong theoretical lenses such as feminist critical theory to do this analysis and generate new data and understandings of the gendered nature of this learn-ing. Much of this feminist work can be characterized as using a critical appraisal strategy to view women's structural oppression through patriarchy.

Clearly community development in Canada has had a critical feminist focus and aspiration, to the point where it would be nearly impossible to find an adult education program that did not have at least part of its pro-gram dedicated to feminist analysis and research.

Conclusion

Of course, it is true that romanticizing Canada is easy; it is definitely a predilection of the Canadian populace to think of ourselves as more socially engaged than our southern neighbor. Yet our roots and our context are dif-ferent, so we have approached our practice and our research differently. Given the discrepancy in population alone (30 million in Canada versus 300 million in the United States), these alternate paths are understandable.

Although the manifesto of Ned Corbett (1943) was written a long time ago, and arguably was not necessarily fulfilled, there is little doubt that the leftist dream that it espoused and embodied continues among those in adult education today. Our Canadian community development sphere has been marked by interest in education for social change. And as has been shown here, the commitment to transformative social movement learning has remained constant over time.

Our perspective on community development can be characterized in four key ways: stress on social movement learning as an integral part of our community development practice, use of media and arts to effect change, a focus on the global scene, and employment of a critical feminist lens to do analysis. Others can benefit from knowing about Canada's track record in community development, how it has evolved, and how it continues. Delv-ing into our practices, historical and present, allows us to show how we do our work here and how it is distinct on the international stage. No one fea-ture of our community development process is unique. Rather, our com-posite format, incorporating our historical influences, learning, media, international dimension, and feminism, makes us distinct. These traits remain defining features of how we research and do community develop-ment in Canada even in this new millennium.

References

Andruske, C. L. "Women's Transitions from Welfare: Where Does That Leave Us?" *Canadian Journal for the Study of Adult Education,* 2001, 15(1), 64–87.

Brigham, S. M., and Walsh, S. C. "The Messiness of Experience: Immigrant Women and an Arts-Informed Research Process." In *Proceedings of the Annual Conference of Cana-dian Association for the Study of Adult Education.* London, ON: University of Western Ontario, 2005.

Butterwick, S., and Selman, J. "Deep Listening in a Feminist Popular Theatre Project: Upsetting the Position of Audience in Participatory Education." *Adult Education Quarterly,* 2003, *54*(1), 7–22.

Canadian Journal for the Study of Adult Education, 2007, *20*(2). Special issue on Work and Lifelong Learning.

Chapman, E. "Adelaide Hoodless." In H. Rouillard (ed.), *Pioneers in Adult Education in Canada.* Toronto: Nelson, 1952.

Ciccarelli, S. B. "ESL for Nation Building." Unpublished master's thesis, Ontario Institute for Studies in Education/University of Toronto, 1999.

Clover, D. E., and Markle, G. "Feminist Arts Practices of Popular Education." *New Zealand Journal of Adult Education,* 2003, *31*(2), 36–52.

Corbett, N. "The Manifesto of the Canadian Association for Adult Education, 1943." In D. Shugurensky (ed.), *History of Education: Selected Moments of the 20th Century.* www.oise.utoronto.ca/research/edu20/moments/1943caae.html.

Duguid, F., Mündel, K., and Shugurensky, D. "Volunteer Work, Informal Learning and the Quest for Sustainable Communities in Canada." *Canadian Journal for the Study of Adult Education,* 2007, *20*(2), 41–56.

English, L. M. "Identity, Hybridity, and Third Space: Complicating the Lives of International Adult Educators." *Convergence,* 2004, *36*(2), 67–80.

English, L. M. "Historical and Contemporary Explorations of the Social Change and Spiritual Directions of Adult Education." *Teachers College Record,* 2005a, *107*(6), 1169–1192.

English, L. M. "Third-Space Practitioners: Women Educating for Civil Society." *Adult Education Quarterly,* 2005b, *55*(2), 85–100.

Friesen, G. "Adult Education and Union Education: Aspects of English Canadian Cultural History in the 20th Century." *Labour/Le Travail,* 1994, *34,* 163–188.

Gouthro, P. "Assessing Power Issues in Canadian and Jamaican Women's Experiences in Learning via Distance in Higher Education." *Teaching in Higher Education,* 2004, *19*(4), 449–461.

Graveline, F. J. "Indigenous Learning." In L. M. English (ed.), *International Encyclopedia of Adult Education.* New York: Palgrave, 2005.

Hall, B. L. *Adult Education and the Development of Socialism in Tanzania.* Kampala: East African Literature Bureau, 1975.

Hall, B. L., and Clover, D. "Social Movement Learning." In L. M. English (ed.), *International Encyclopedia of Adult Education.* New York: Palgrave, 2005.

Liu, L. W. "Unveiling the Invisible Learning from Unpaid Household Work: Chinese Immigrants' Perspectives." *Canadian Journal for the Study of Adult Education,* 2007, *20*(2), 25–40.

Lotz, J., and Welton, M. R. *Father Jimmy: The Life and Times of Father Jimmy.* Wreck Cove, NS: Breton Books, 1997.

Maitra, S., and Shan, H. "Informal Learning of Highly Educated Immigrant Women in Contingent Work." In *Proceedings of the Annual Conference of Canadian Association for the Study of Adult Education.* London, ON: University of Western Ontario, 2005.

Miles, A. *Integrative Feminisms: 1960s-1990s.* New York: Routledge, 1995.

Miles, A. "Feminist Perspectives on Globalization and Integrative Transformative Learning." In E. V. O'Sullivan, A. Morrell, and M. A. O'Connor (eds.), *Expanding the Boundaries of Transformative Learning.* New York: Palgrave, 2002.

Mirchandani, K. "Immigrants Matter: Canada's Social Agenda on Skill and Learning." *Convergence,* 2004, *37*(1), 61–68.

Mojab, S. "The Power of Economic Globalization: Deskilling Immigrant Women Through Training." In R. M. Cervero and A. L. Wilson (eds.), *Power in Practice: Adult Education and Struggle for Knowledge and Power in Society.* San Francisco: Jossey-Bass, 2000.

Neal, R. *Brotherhood Economics: Women and Co-Operatives in Nova Scotia.* Sydney, NS: University College of Cape Breton Press, 1998.

O'Sullivan, E. *Transformative Learning: Educational Vision for the 21st Century.* New York: Zed Books, 1999.

Roy, C. *The Raging Grannies: Wild Hats, Cheeky Songs, and Witty Actions for a Better World.* Montreal: Black Rose Books, 2004.

Roy, C. "Learning the World and Building a Sense of Community While Watching the Silver Screen: Community Education Through Documentary Film Festivals." Paper presented at What's Working in Community Development Conference, Acadia University, Wolfville, NS, June 25, 2008.

Ryan, M., and English, L. M. "A Growth-Centered Approach to Women's Development in Grenada." *Community Development Journal,* 2004, *39*(1), 38–48.

Selman, G., Cooke, M., Selman, M., and Dampier, P. *The Foundations of Adult Education in Canada.* (2nd ed.) Toronto: Thompson Educational Publishing, 1998.

Slade, B., Luo, Y., and Schugurensky, D. "Seeking 'Canadian Experience': The Informal Learning of New Immigrants as Volunteer Workers." In *Proceedings of the Annual Conference of the Canadian Association for the Study of Adult Education.* London, ON: University of Western Ontario, 2005.

United Nations. *Community Development and National Development: A Report by a Committee Appointed by the Secretary General of the United Nations.* New York: United Nations, 1963.

Walter, P. "Adult Learning in New Social Movements: Environmental Protest and the Struggle for the Clayoquot Sound Rainforest." *Adult Education Quarterly,* 2007, *57*(3), 248–263.

Walter, P. "Through a Gender Lens: Explaining Northeastern Thai Women's Participation in Adult Literacy Education." *International Journal of Lifelong Education,* 2004, *23*(5), 423–441.

Welton, M. R. (ed.). *Knowledge for the People: The Struggle for Adult Learning in English-Speaking Canada, 1828–1973.* Toronto: Ontario Institute for the Studies in Education Press, 1987.

Welton, M. R. *Little Mosie from the Margaree: A Biography of Moses Michael Coady.* Toronto: Thompson Educational Publishers, 2001.

LEONA M. ENGLISH is professor of adult education at St. Francis Xavier University in Antigonish, Nova Scotia.

The authors speak broadly to how the preceding chapters contribute to a description of the Canadian mosaic of adult education. They point also to further reading, as well as remaining questions about the uniqueness of our nation's field.

Reaching Out Across the Border

Leona M. English, Patricia Cranton

When Canadian folk singer Joni Mitchell (1990) sang the line, "I wish I had a river to skate away on," on a popular song, she captured a quintessential Canadian image. Her reference to winter sports and cold temperatures is very much a Canadian one, given the ways in which weather and vast geography have defined us as a nation and helped shape adult education's particular interests in distance education, community development, and rural education. We are a relatively new (confederation in 1867) and small (about 33 million people) country, still shaped by our colonial past with Britain and France, a rocky relationship with its First Peoples, and the sometimes testy bond with the elephant next door, the United States, our largest trading partner. How our nation's development affects our field has been broached by a number of writers in this volume, including Elizabeth Lange and Aaron Chubb (Chapter Six), as well as Donovan Plumb (Chapter One). As the previous chapters have shown, we have evidenced in our practice an interest in civil society through health and literacy work, community development, and environmental education. Our history has been peppered with cases of innovative initiatives to reach participants in areas as disparate as the Far North and eastern Nova Scotia. These innovations have become hallmarks of how we practice in our field and manifest our various commitments to the greater good. Yet our challenges have been greater. We have had linguistic issues as in Quebec and in the Far North and continue to try to include our ever-growing population of new Canadians in our programs, services, and vision. It has not always been easy. Although our medical system is the envy of much of the Western world, internally we question whether it is eroding and whether our educational initiatives are strong

enough for our citizens to cope with issues of access to this system, especially those who have low incomes and low literacy. Although our history of care and inclusivity is strong, we constantly ask if we have moved away from our most cherished ideals toward a more institutionally driven and exclusive practice of adult education. As we have become more professionalized and developed, we may have forgotten some of our commitment to those most in need and marginalized. Yet we assert our uniqueness in our Canadian way of doing and seeing things in adult education, a uniqueness that is sometimes hard to recognize when we consider our many connections to our American neighbors. And that is to be expected given our shared land mass and our entwined economies, not to mention the flooding of our airwaves by American media. Here, north of the forty-ninth parallel, the American presidential inauguration of Barack Obama was big news, and our national newspapers, the *National Post* and the *Globe and Mail,* and large urban papers like the *Montreal Gazette* and the *Toronto Star* were perhaps more interested in the 2008 U.S. election than our own Canadian election. There is no doubt we share a great deal, yet we have distinctive differences, even among and between parts of our own country, as shown in the chapters that look at Quebec, the North, and eastern Canada.

As citizens, we are mindful that our field does not operate apart from our country's larger conversations and debates. Our discussion is stimulated by the recent publication of *A Fair Country* (2008) by the intellectual Jean Ralston Saul. Saul argues that Canada is indeed a distinct society and is strongly influenced by our Aboriginal background—according to him we are a "metis civilization" (p. 3)—set apart and shaped by Aboriginal ideas such as egalitarianism, a proper balance between individual and group, and a penchant for negotiation over violence. In Saul's view, our imbibing these values has resulted in a citizenry that has been since its inception concerned about "peace, welfare, and good government" (p. 169), though we have not always articulated it in this way. His point is that a collaborative, consensual, and congenial decision-making process has been learned from our First Nations people and has been important to our formation as a country; it makes us distinct in the Western world. Some of the chapter in this volume show an orientation to such collaboration, as in the community development chapters by English (Chapter Eight) and MacKeracher (Chapter Three) and our opening chapter by Plumb. Yet clearly many of these examples are historical, and those at the grassroots in areas such as literacy know that we have not always been faithful to our forebears' example. If Saul is right, we have quite a challenge ahead to learn more about our Aboriginal roots and how it is that we can become more of who we were intended to be.

In this volume, we have spoken to a primarily American audience about who we are as adult educators. In addition to the collaborative orientation named by Saul (2008) and shown by many of the chapter authors, researchers such as Quigley, Coady, Grégoire, Folinsbee, and Kraglund-Gauthier highlight in Chapter Five a concern in this country for social issues such as how one's overall well-being affects literacy and learning. They have shown how federal monies have sponsored research into the multiple determinants of health (for example, economics, geography, and social class) and how we might improve them to have a more holistic approach to learning. Although we occasionally have national debates about health care, the great consensus is that it needs to be improved if the overall welfare and education of our citizens are to be maintained or increased.

We might also tell our American colleagues that we have a particular concern for the education of our First Nations people. Robinson shows in Chapter Two the creative use of media to address learning and education challenges among them. The fact that we include a chapter on this population in this volume, and that many other Canadian publications do, is an indication of our concern. Yet we notice that Aboriginal issues rarely, if ever, have a presence in American adult education literature. This may be more a factor of percentage of population and the reality that our colleagues are concerned with other groups such as African Americans.

In conversation with American colleagues, we inevitably end up discussing the linguistic issue and how our field has been influenced by attention to French issues and contributions. As Hrimech notes in Chapter Four, our government policy of bilingualism has helped to shape our field, our emphases, and our direction. Yet we admit that our national association, the Canadian Association for the Study of Adult Education, has few French participants and our academic journals and publications are primarily written in English. That said, our federal government policies on instruction in French have remained a constant, albeit minor, presence in our writing and practice. Perhaps the "two solitudes" (French and English cultures) (MacLennan, 1945) are a fallacy.

Americans might also be interested to note that quite related to our historical past is our continuing interest with social movement learning, a theme that winds through three chapters in this volume—Lange and Chubb on environmental education; MacKeracher on sites such as the Antigonish movement, Frontier College, and Farm Radio; and Plumb on critical turns and discourses. The attention to learning as an aspect of social movements has been continuously accentuated and become an integral part of our practice. As a field, we are concerned with drawing our learners into the larger social issues of our day. Consequently, labor market and human resource discourse is not as strong an element in our adult education research as in other jurisdictions. We would likely hold, admittedly with a degree of pride, that adult education in Canada has given strong attention to the common good, as articulated in every chapter in this volume. There is much evidence from these authors that attention has continued despite recession and sometimes regressive government policy.

Yet we are aware of the danger of creating stereotypes of Canada and its people even if it is part of a legitimate process of describing or articulating who we are. We could easily fall into the trap of becoming the Hollywood version of our country, replete with Mounties, beavers, snowy mountain-tops, and wilderness. And at some level, we have enjoyed these stereotypes because they have glamorized us and made us distinct from Americans (Berton, 1997). Yet a close examination of the chapters in this volume will show a more critical reading of our practice that goes beyond these carica-tures. Robinson and Hrimech, for instance, explore at length in, respectively, Chapters Two and Four, the complexities of educational work in the North and in Quebec, respectively.

Despite its ineffable quality, we are sure that there is a continued "Cana-dianness" about our field. Our colleagues from the United Kingdom and the United States frequently mention this when we meet them at conferences, yet it is a struggle to say exactly what that is. Both of us have lived in the United States, and we too struggle to name that uniqueness. But we know that it is there.

Resources

Much of our adult education literature and our movements have originated from our government-funded universities, in particular from those that offer master's and doctoral degrees in adult education. These include the Uni-versity of British Columbia, University of Alberta, Athabasca University, The Ontario Institute for Studies in Education (OISE)/University of Toronto, University of New Brunswick, and St. Francis Xavier University. We have come a long way since Florence O'Neill (graduated in 1944) and Roby Kidd (graduated 1947) had to cross the border to attend Columbia University in New York City in order to earn their doctorates in adult education.

Perhaps it is our academic and adult education texts that truly reveal what we have been interested in here in Canada. A Canadian Association for the Study of Adult Education listserv discussion in fall 2008 about the best textbook to use for an introductory course in adult education revealed the ways in which we as a field are sometimes uncertain about our identity (some respondents chose American books) and the ways in which we are very clear that we are unique (the majority of respondents insisted we use Canadian books in our classes). The discussion highlighted our ambivalence about asserting ourselves strongly as a distinct field in a distinct country. Some journals and books that surfaced in that discussion and while we were editing this volume are noted here as suggestions for further reading on Canadian adult education.

Journals
Canadian Journal for the Study of Adult Education (CJSAE), our major aca-demic journal in adult education. This journal publishes essays and reviews, mainly from Canadian writers and academics. It was established in the early 1980s to showcase Canadian adult education history, debate current ideas, and review our scholars' publications. Supported by CASAE, the CJSAE is

released twice yearly and is edited by Tom Nesbit at Simon Fraser University in British Columbia.

Journal of Distance Education, which publishes the work of adult educators who have concentrated on distance teaching and learning; supported by the Canadian Network for Innovation in Education, previously known as the Canadian Association for Distance Education. This journal is published twice yearly and is edited by Mark Bullen at the British Columbia Institute of Technology.

Canadian Journal of Higher Education, sponsored by the Pan-Canadian Society for Studies in Higher Education. This journal publishes papers concerning teaching and learning in universities, community colleges, and other institutions of higher education. It is housed at McGill University in Montreal.

Books

Barer-Stein, T., and Kompf, M. (eds.). *The Craft of Teaching Adults.* (3rd ed.) Toronto: Irwin, 2001. This book is a collection of essays on Canada by Canadians. Although somewhat dated, it provides a solid introduction to the major writers and interests in Canada and includes chapters by seminal figures in our field's development, such as Alan Thomas, Roby Kidd, and James Draper.

Fenwick, T., Nesbit, T., and Spencer, B. (eds.), *Contexts of Adult Education: Canadian Perspectives.* Toronto: Thompson Educational Publishing, 2006. *Contexts* is a collection of essays on various themes in Canadian adult education with contributions from most active writers in the field in Canada. Sponsored by the CASAE, the editors challenged writers to articulate a Canadian way of thinking and being in adult education. Attention is given to areas of research as varied as the economy, philosophy, critical theory, and First Nations education. There is a deliberate attempt to identify Canadian writers and research on each topic, making this book an invaluable resource for those interested Canadian adult education.

MacKeracher, D. *Making Sense of Adult Learning.* (2nd ed.) Toronto: University of Toronto Press, 2004. This book represents a strong introduction to adult learning and is produced by one of the foremothers of our academic field of adult education, Dorothy MacKeracher, author of Chapter Three in this volume. This text grew out of her collaborations with professors such as Don Brundage at OISE when she was a doctoral student in the 1970s. She concerns herself with learning principles and emotions in learning, and incorporates the spirituality of learning and facilitating in the text.

Poonwassi, D. H., and Poonwassie, A. (eds.). *Fundamentals of Adult Education in Canada: Issues and Practices for Lifelong Learning.* Toronto: Thompson Educational Publishing, 2001. The authors are Manitoba-based adult educators who have brought together a collection of Canadian writers to explore our history, field, and future in adult education. Their book contains a number of informative chapters on Canadian adult education and is

New Directions for Adult and Continuing Education • DOI: 10.1002/ace

crowned by a seminal essay from historian of adult education Gordon Selman, who examines the stages of adult education in Canada.

Selman, G., Cooke, M., Selman, M., and Dampier, P. *The Foundations of Adult Education in Canada.* (2nd ed.) Toronto: Thompson Educational Publishing, 1998. This foundational text in adult education covers our history, philosophy, writing, and policy. This is an ambitious book from a significant historian of adult education (G. Selman), which attempts to canvass the field, its practices, and its distinctiveness. No bonafide study of Canadian adult education would be possible without this book.

Welton, M. R. *Little Mosie from the Margaree: A Biography of Moses Michael Coady.* Toronto: Thompson Educational Publishing, 2001. This biography is important to the Canadian field of adult education because it not only profiles the life and times of Moses Coady, one of the leaders of the Antigonish movement, but also sets him in his historical and cultural landscape, from the 1920s to 1950s, when the field of adult education was coming of age in this country. In this important and original work, Welton traces the many important influences on the Roman Catholic priest's life and times, shedding light in the process on our field's interests and preoccupations over time.

References

Berton, P. "Hollywood's Canada: The Americanization of our National Image." In E. Cameron (ed.), *Canadian Culture.* Toronto: Canadian Scholars' Press, 1997.
MacLennan, H. *Two Solitudes.* Toronto: MacMillan, 1945.
Mitchell, J. "River" (song). Blue (compact disc). Originally released 1971. Reprise, Warner Brothers Music, 1990.
Saul, J. R. *A Fair Country: Telling Truths About Canada.* Toronto: Viking, 2008.

LEONA M. ENGLISH *is professor of adult education at St. Francis Xavier University in Antigonish, Nova Scotia.*

PATRICIA CRANTON *is professor of adult education at Penn State University Harrisburg.*

INDEX

Dampier, P., 85–87, 98
Dawson, A., 67–68
DDT, 64
De Souza, M., 62
Declaration of Alma-Ata (1978), 52
Delaney, I., 30
Dene First Nations, 16, 20
Dennison, J. D., 74
Department of Continuing Education, Canada, 75
Department of Industry, Canada, 30; Division of Handicrafts, 30
Department of Post-Secondary Education and Labour, Canada, 75
Devine, G., 5, 6
Division of Handicrafts (Department of Industry, Canada), 30
Douglas, Tommy, 51
Doyle, Sister Irene, 30, 86
Draper, J., 7, 97
Duguid, F., 65, 87

Earth Day, 64
Educational success, theme of, 21
Edwards, R., 11
"End of History," 6
English, L. M., 11, 83, 85, 86, 88–89, 93, 94
English, Mabel, 20
Environmental adult education (EAE): antecedents and Canadian approaches to, 63–66; Canada's historical context for, 62–63; and funding, structure, and PIRG student movements, 67–69; and nonformal adult education, 66–67; and student environmental activism, 61–70
Environmental Adult Education: From Awareness to Action (UNESCO), 65
Environmental Education for Sustainable Societies and Global Responsibility, 64
Epp, J., 52, 62, 63
Epp Report, 52. *See also* "Achieving Health for All: A Framework for Health Promotion" (Epp)

Fair Country, A (Saul), 94
Family, theme of, 20–21
Farm Radio Forum study groups, 28, 83, 85, 95
Farmers' Union of Canada, 32
Federated Women's Institutes of Ontario, 28
Feminism, 10–11

Fenwick, T., 11, 97
First Nations, 20, 83, 94, 95
Fitzpatrick, A., 26, 27
Fogo, New Foundland, 87
Fogo Process, 17
Folinsbee, S., 49, 50, 53, 54, 56, 57, 94
Follen, S., 66
Fonder l'avenir: le temps de la conciliation (Bouchard and Taylor), 44
Food Not Bombs, 67
Foundations of Adult Education in Canada (Selman, Cooke, Selman, and Dampier), 98
France, 8
Francisation, 42, 43
Freire, P., 17, 18, 78
French language, 37, 95; preservation of, in Quebec, 41–42
French population, 61
Friesen, G., 85
Frontier College, 26–27, 33, 83, 95
Fukuyama, F., 6
Fundamentals of Adult Education in Canada: Issues and Practice for Lifelong Learning (Poonwassie and Poonwassie), 97

Gardner, B., 55, 56
Georgeault, P., 41
Germany, 39
Ginn, J., 55
Giroux, H., 17, 18
Globe and Mail, 94
Gouthro, P., 11, 88–89
Government of the Northwest Territories, Education, Culture and Employment, 16
Grace, A., 7, 11
Graveline, F. J., 89
Great Britain, 6, 7, 11, 26, 28, 93
Great Depression, 85
Greenpeace, 64
Grégoire, H., 49, 50, 53, 54, 56, 57, 94
Grenada, 88–89
Grimm, K., 66
Grolier Hall, 21
Gruenwald, D., 66
Guelph, Ontario, 27
Gwich'in people, 16

Habermas, J., 10
Halfacre-Hitchcock, A., 67, 69
Hall, B. L., 26, 33, 63, 64, 66, 86, 87

NEW DIRECTIONS FOR ADULT AND CONTINUING EDUCATION
ORDER FORM SUBSCRIPTION AND SINGLE ISSUES

DISCOUNTED BACK ISSUES:

Use this form to receive 20% off all back issues of *New Directions for Adult and Continuing Education*.
All single issues priced at **$23.20** (normally $29.00)

TITLE	ISSUE NO.	ISBN
_____	_____	_____
_____	_____	_____
_____	_____	_____

Call 888-378-2537 or see mailing instructions below. When calling, mention the promotional code JBXND
to receive your discount. For a complete list of issues, please visit www.josseybass.com/go/ndace

SUBSCRIPTIONS: (1 YEAR, 4 ISSUES)

☐ New Order   ☐ Renewal

U.S.	☐ Individual: $89	☐ Institutional: $244
CANADA/MEXICO	☐ Individual: $89	☐ Institutional: $284
ALL OTHERS	☐ Individual: $113	☐ Institutional: $318

Call 888-378-2537 or see mailing and pricing instructions below.
Online subscriptions are available at www.interscience.wiley.com

ORDER TOTALS:

Issue / Subscription Amount: $ _____

Shipping Amount: $ _____
(for single issues only – subscription prices include shipping)

Total Amount: $ _____

SHIPPING CHARGES:		
SURFACE	DOMESTIC	CANADIAN
First Item	$5.00	$6.00
Each Add'l Item	$3.00	$1.50

(No sales tax for U.S. subscriptions. Canadian residents, add GST for subscription orders. Individual rate subscriptions must
be paid by personal check or credit card. Individual rate subscriptions may not be resold as library copies.)

BILLING & SHIPPING INFORMATION:

☐ **PAYMENT ENCLOSED:** *(U.S. check or money order only. All payments must be in U.S. dollars.)*

☐ **CREDIT CARD:**   ☐VISA   ☐MC   ☐AMEX

Card number _____ Exp. Date_____

Card Holder Name_____ Card Issue # *(required)* _____

Signature _____ Day Phone_____

☐ **BILL ME:** *(U.S. institutional orders only. Purchase order required.)*

Purchase order # _____
Federal Tax ID 13559302 • GST 89102-8052

Name_____

Address_____

Phone_____ E-mail_____

Copy or detach page and send to: **John Wiley & Sons, PTSC, 5th Floor**
989 Market Street, San Francisco, CA 94103-1741

Order Form can also be faxed to: **888-481-2665**

PROMO JBXND

UNITED STATES POSTAL SERVICE ®

Statement of Ownership, Management, and Circulation
(All Periodicals Publications Except Requester Publications)

1. Publication Title	2. Publication Number							3. Filing Date
New Directions for Adult and Continuing Education	1	0	5	2 _	2	8	9 1	10/1/2009

4. Issue Frequency	5. Number of Issues Published Annually	6. Annual Subscription Price
Quarterly	4	$89

7. Complete Mailing Address of Known Office of Publication *(Not printer) (Street, city, county, state, and ZIP+4®)*

Wiley Subscription Services, Inc. at Jossey-Bass, 989 Market St., San Francisco, CA 94103

Contact Person
Joe Schuman
Telephone *(Include area code)*
415-487-9838

8. Complete Mailing Address of Headquarters or General Business Office of Publisher *(Not printer)*

Wiley Subscription Services, Inc. 111 River Street, Hoboken, NJ 07030

9. Full Names and Complete Mailing Addresses of Publisher, Editor, and Managing Editor *(Do not leave blank)*

Publisher *(Name and complete mailing address)*

Wiley Subscription Services, Inc., A Wiley Company at San Francisco, 989 Market St., San Francisco, CA 94103-1741

Editor *(Name and complete mailing address)*

Susan Imel, Ohio State University/Eric-Acve, 1900 Kenny Road, Columbus, OH 43210-1090

Managing Editor *(Name and complete mailing address)*

Co-editor - Jovita M. Ross-Gordon, Texas State University, EAPS Department, San Marcos, TX 78666

10. Owner *(Do not leave blank. If the publication is owned by a corporation, give the name and address of the corporation immediately followed by the names and addresses of all stockholders owning or holding 1 percent or more of the total amount of stock. If not owned by a corporation, give the names and addresses of the individual owners. If owned by a partnership or other unincorporated firm, give its name and address as well as those of each individual owner. If the publication is published by a nonprofit organization, give its name and address.)*

Full Name	Complete Mailing Address
Wiley Subscription Services, Inc.	111 River Street, Hoboken, NJ 07030
(see attached list)	

11. Known Bondholders, Mortgagees, and Other Security Holders Owning or Holding 1 Percent or More of Total Amount of Bonds, Mortgages, or Other Securities. If none, check box ──▶ ☑ None

Full Name	Complete Mailing Address

12. Tax Status *(For completion by nonprofit organizations authorized to mail at nonprofit rates) (Check one)*
The purpose, function, and nonprofit status of this organization and the exempt status for federal income tax purposes:
☐ Has Not Changed During Preceding 12 Months
☐ Has Changed During Preceding 12 Months *(Publisher must submit explanation of change with this statement)*

PS Form **3526,** September 2007 *(Page 1 of 3 (Instructions Page 3))* PSN 7530-01-000-9931 PRIVACY NOTICE: See our privacy policy on www.usps.com

13. Publication Title	14. Issue Date for Circulation Data Below
New Directions for Adult and Continuing Education	Summer 2009

15. Extent and Nature of Circulation			Average No. Copies Each Issue During Preceding 12 Months	No. Copies of Single Issue Published Nearest to Filing Date
a. Total Number of Copies *(Net press run)*			1149	1124
b. Paid Circulation *(By Mail and Outside the Mail)*	(1)	Mailed Outside-County Paid Subscriptions Stated on PS Form 3541(Include paid distribution above nominal rate, advertiser's proof copies, and exchange copies)	381	359
	(2)	Mailed In-County Paid Subscriptions Stated on PS Form 3541 (Include paid distribution above nominal rate, advertiser's proof copies, and exchange copies)	0	0
	(3)	Paid Distribution Outside the Mails Including Sales Through Dealers and Carriers, Street Vendors, Counter Sales, and Other Paid Distribution Outside USPS®	0	0
	(4)	Paid Distribution by Other Classes of Mail Through the USPS (e.g. First-Class Mail®)	0	0
c. Total Paid Distribution *(Sum of 15b (1), (2), (3), and (4))*			381	359
d. Free or Nominal Rate Distribution *(By Mail and Outside the Mail)*	(1)	Free or Nominal Rate Outside-County Copies Included on PS Form 3541	30	30
	(2)	Free or Nominal Rate In-County Copies Included on PS Form 3541	0	0
	(3)	Free or Nominal Rate Copies Mailed at Other Classes Through the USPS (e.g. First-Class Mail)	0	0
	(4)	Free or Nominal Rate Distribution Outside the Mail (Carriers or other means)	0	0
e. Total Free or Nominal Rate Distribution *(Sum of 15d (1), (2), (3) and (4))*			30	30
f. Total Distribution *(Sum of 15c and 15e)*		▶	411	389
g. Copies not Distributed *(See Instructions to Publishers #4 (page #3))*		▶	738	735
h. Total *(Sum of 15f and g)*		▶	1149	1124
i. Percent Paid *(15c divided by 15f times 100)*		▶	92%	92%

16. Publication of Statement of Ownership

☐ If the publication is a general publication, publication of this statement is required. Will be printed in the Winter 2009 issue of this publication. ☐ Publication not required.

17. Signature and Title of Editor, Publisher, Business Manager, or Owner

Susan E. Lewis, VP & Publisher - Periodicals

Date
10/1/2009

I certify that all information furnished on this form is true and complete. I understand that anyone who furnishes false or misleading information on this form or who omits material or information requested on the form may be subject to criminal sanctions (including fines and imprisonment) and/or civil sanctions (including civil penalties).

PS Form **3526,** September 2007 *(Page 2 of 3)*